The "Business" of Sewing

How to Start, Maintain and Achieve Success

By Barbara Wright Sykes

COLLINS PUBLICATIONS
Chino Hills, CA U.S.A

The "Business" of Sewing
How to Start, Maintain and Achieve Success
By Barbara Wright Sykes

Published by: COLLINS PUBLICATIONS
3233 Grand Avenue, Suite N-294
Chino Hills, CA 91709-1318 U.S.A

Cover Design by David Hughes
Illustrations by Ken Clubb
Photography by David Shea
Layout and Design by Carrie Florer
Edited by: Laura Harrison-Tull
             Barry Hamdani
             Carrie Florer

Publisher's Cataloging in Publication
    (Prepared by Quality Books Inc.)

Wright Sykes, Barbara, 1947-
    The "Business" Of Sewing: How to Start, Maintain, and Achieve Success /
By Barbara Wright Sykes.
    p. cm.
    Includes bibliographical references and index.
    Preassigned LCCN: 92-81282.
    ISBN 0-9632857-5-0

    1.Clothing trade—Management. 2.New business enterprises—
Handbooks, manuals, etc. I Title.

TT497.S9 1992   687.068
                         QB192-10461

DEDICATED TO...

My family—my parents Mattie and Percy, and my step-father James, my daughters Tiffany and Adrienne, and most of all to my loving husband and manager, Fletcher.

ACKNOWLEDGEMENTS

A special thanks to the library staff at Chino, Claremont, Ontario Main, and Ontario South; Karen Kunkel, Education Manager of McCalls Pattern Co., Patricia Nilson, Vice President of Retail Development at Simplicity Pattern Co, Linda Turner Greipentrog, Editor of Sew News, and to Sylvia Miller, Publications Director, Barry and Arlys Hamdani, Publishers of Hamdani Communications, and to the staff at Flo's #2, and Kaiser (Claremont). I would like to express my gratitude to the many individuals who shared, contributed, supported and gave so unselfishly of themselves:

ANNETTE SCHOFIELD
ARTHUR WINN
BARBARA GONZALES
BETH MAURO
BILL DALEY
CARRIE FLORER
DAN POYNTER
DAWN SCHOEFF
DR. DONALD DOSSEY
DR. MARSHALL REDDICK
ELIZABETH BRODEUR
FRANZ WAGENBACK
GAIL BYRD TAYLOR
JANE HOFFMAN
JOAN ALLEN
JOEL SANDERS
JULIE DAVEY
KATHLEEN SPIKE
LAURA HARRISON-TULL
LINDA BAKER
LINDA JOHNS
LISA WHITE
MARY JANE McCLELLAND
NANCY ZIEMAN
PAULINE POWELL
PENNY B. MARINO
PHIL CROCFER
SHAWN MICHALKA
STACEY D'AMATO
VIVIANNE WIGHTMAN

CONTENTS

A Word from Nancy Zieman...

Turning a love of sewing into a financially profitable venture can be a dream come true, yet it can also pose many new and sometimes perplexing challenges. Barbara's comprehensive book is a real confidence builder for the novice, offering advice on the many facets of organizing, managing, and marketing a sewing business.

The "Business" of Sewing gives you the benefit of Barbara's experience, as she advises you on how to develop a business plan, obtain funding, establish a pricing structure, maintain a professional image, and solve problems. She includes a variety of sample forms and charts which can be adapted to meet individual needs. She obviously enjoys what she is doing, and she shares a wealth of information which can guide the beginner over the rough spots.

— **Nancy Zieman**
Hostess of *Sewing With Nancy*
and owner of Nancy's Notions, a sewing
notions mail order catalog company

FOREWARD

The professionally orientated seamstress has been waiting for *The "Business" Of Sewing*. The fast growing and respected cottage industry of custom clothiers now has a resource to help answer questions and direct expanding businesses.

This book systematically outlines the steps taken to start up an otherwise only dreamed about home sewing business. But more importantly, knowledge is provided on acquiring that critically important "professionalism and self-commitment" necessary to succeed in the couture, custom sewing business.

— **Penny B. Marino**
Associate Professor, Chaffey College
Fashion Merchandising and Design

"Business vs. Hobby"

Business Basics

INTRODUCTION

There are a number of qualified individuals who are extremely talented when it comes to sewing. They possess talents that lie dormant in the market place, resulting from lack of knowledge or the courage to strike out on their own and start a business as a sewing professional.

Starting and maintaining a successful sewing business is no deep, dark secret known only to those who actually own successful sewing businesses. While you may feel this way due to the many questions that you have; questions such as: (1) How do I start my own business? (2) How much money will I need? (3) Where will I obtain the funds? (4) How will I price my services? and (5) Where will I get my customers? The list grows as you further consider the process.

There is good news! The foundation of this book was built upon addressing the needs of individuals such as yourself. The answers to the previous questions and many more will be found in this text. Step-by-step solutions to reveal the policies, practices and procedures to a successful sewing business are yours. Let's get started!

KNOWING WHEN YOU ARE READY

Have you scheduled your cost of living raise for this year? How about the vacation you so richly deserve? Working for yourself gives you unlimited opportunity to enjoy life! However, along with the wealth of benefits comes an equal share of responsibility. You have the responsibility to start, maintain, and become successful. This may sound like a tremendous undertaking. Relax, you already have one of the most important elements...DESIRE.

The next step is to become relentless in the determination to achieve your goal. To facilitate the process, you must clearly understand your motivation for going into business. Simply ask yourself why you want to go into business, and be honest with your answers. We will discuss setting goals in more detail in Chapter Three "*Starting Your Business.*"

When interviewed, many sewing professionals stated that they chose to go into business because it afforded them the opportunity to have control over their own time. This was of great importance to those who had small children. Some stated that financial independence was their main motivation. Others maintained that they simply loved sewing with a passion, and being in a sewing business allowed them the luxury to utilize their creative talents and receive monetary rewards for doing so.

No matter what your motivation for going into business, the final and most important step is to acquire the proper knowledge to make your goal a reality. You must research every aspect of your business. This is commonly referred to as "doing your homework." Gaining sufficient knowledge will allow you to make intelligent decisions regarding your business.

As a sewing professional, you must stay abreast of current trends in your field, and create your own research and development system by reading everything related to your business. In addition, you will need to surround yourself with successful individuals who are involved in business endeavors such as yours. Become inquisitive as to how they achieved success. You will be surprised to learn that most successful people love to share knowledge with others. Remember that knowledge is power, and by employing these key elements, success will be yours!

This brings you to the point where you must ask yourself if you are ready to go into business.

How do you know when you are absolutely ready? Have you ever decided to do something and actually got excited about it? Without your knowledge, somewhere out of the blue, a little voice said, "That's a good idea; but...?" This is the voice of self-doubt taking control, causing you to give up what could be a perfectly good idea.

Examine this situation. You finally are able to put to rest that annoying little voice and move on to actually outlining the various steps to launching your business. Then, you come across a certain element, say pricing for example, and you simply panic. Once again, the voice of self-doubt returns. This time, self-doubt is <u>really</u> playing with your mind. It is saying to you, "You couldn't possibly think of charging for what you do, because you don't know how; and no one will pay you what you are worth!"

Last, but certainly not least, you successfully arrive at the place in your planning where you are ready to obtain your business license. You are in your car circling for ten minutes to find a parking space. Finally, you get to the business license section, only to get the most unfriendly clerk in creation. Now you are absolutely convinced...the little voice of self-doubt was right.

Wrong! In fact, nothing could be further from the truth! When you find yourself experiencing self-doubt, it is time to exercise all the will-power you possess to overcome the temptation that so many people experience—giving in to self-doubt and lack of confidence.

At this juncture in your growth and development process, you must employ what is commonly referred to as the out-of-body experience. This means actually stepping back and talking to yourself to instill the fact that you are worthy. No one said it would be without some difficulty. Keep in mind, no matter what degree of difficulty or area of deficiency you are experiencing, *you will overcome* it through gaining sufficient knowledge.

When you exercise your ability to institute this theory, you will overcome self-doubt; giving you the opportunity to move past *any* obstacle.

Another primary reason why this theory is so crucial is that not only will you face self-doubt, you will receive negative advice from people who only dream. Those individuals will equate your self-worth and ability to accomplish goals with theirs, which is limited only to dreams. You know—the people who always tell you what you *should* do!

Before considering the advice of others, take a mental inventory of their accomplishments as well as their qualifications to give such advice. Always investigate the subject matter for yourself. You will only gain more knowledge. Keep in mind that knowledge is power, and the more you acquire, the more successful you will become.

Never lose sight of the fact that you must always believe in yourself. Become your biggest fan. This will allow you the conviction to say to yourself, "I am prepared to face the challenges that business has to offer!"

Let's take a look at how *The "Business" Of Sewing* can assist you in accomplishing your goals.

Over the years, the sewing industry has experienced tremendous growth. Several prominent factors have had significant influence on this trend:

Increased consumer demands for custom made clothing, sewing for special needs (such as the handicapped) and home-decor; not to mention advanced technology within the industry, as well as the increased interest on the part of sewing enthusiasts and students to become professional.

The upsurge in the industries' growth curve created a need for extensive research, which revealed a number of concerns of significant importance to various segments of the industry.

The groups that have been most concerned are sewing teachers and students, sewing enthusiasts and professionals, and the end users of goods and services of the sewing industry—the clients and the consumers.

How can *The "Business" Of Sewing* be of benefit to you in achieving your goals? The book takes a realistic look at the various concerns that individuals face going into business, and those issues associated with individuals in business who experience difficulty.

Not only does the book examine these issues, it offers ways to resolve the problems associated with being in a sewing profession.

The book is designed for several important groups: sewing professionals, home-sewers, students and teachers, and the clients who will utilize their services. Let's examine how *The "Business" Of Sewing* applies to each group.

SEWING PROFESSIONALS

A significant number of sewing professionals experience difficulty in starting and maintaining their businesses. The cause of the difficulty is largely due to lack of knowledge with regard to client interaction, poor business and time management, insufficient skill level, lack of proper recordkeeping, and the fear of failure associated with such an endeavor.

The problems can be overwhelming. The need to see others in the sewing profession who have experienced similar difficulties, and yet succeeded in spite of those challenges, is of great importance.

The "Business" Of Sewing addresses the above issues as well as how to handle doubt, fear and procrastination. It also offers solid methods to assist you in overcoming those obstacles.

HOME-SEWERS

Over the years, there have been increasing demands on the part of home-sewers to start their own businesses, much of which has been brought on by the need to stay at home to raise their families and contribute to the family unit while doing so. What better way to accomplish both goals than to have a home-based business, one that takes very little start-up capital?

There was a time when home-sewers were thought of as dowdy little housewives who stayed home to take care of the family, and engaged in sewing as a hobby. Women across America have put that myth to shame.

The home-sewer of today is educated and knowledgeable regarding the latest technological advances in the field of sewing. She possesses state-of-the-art sewing machines and sergers, notions and supplies, in addition to having a warehouse full of fashion fabrics! She is detail-oriented, and she takes great pride in the fact that she is one of many who are classified as a home-sewer.

How did this phenomenon get started? The '60s found women no longer satisfied with standing in the shadows of men. Ignited with the spirit of change, women banded together to make a statement. Thus came the birth of the women's Equal Rights Movement.

Firmly rooted in their beliefs, more and more women found themselves retiring their aprons, losing interest in daytime TV, and whisking their little ones off to day care to assume their rightful positions as home-sewing professionals.

The '70s found the pioneers of the women's movement restless and dissatisfied with corporate America. Many qualified women were consistently overlooked for promotional consideration, not to mention the blatant discrepancy on the part of salaries paid to women in comparison to their male counterparts. Given those circumstances, after having children, many women found it to be advantageous to have their own businesses as home-sewing professionals.

A 9-to-5 job no longer satisfied their senses of

self-worth. A new agenda surfaced—one calling for financial independence, self-accomplishment, upward mobility; and a home-based sewing business was the answer.

Women from coast to coast, armed and equipped with the knowledge, experience, and the art of business, decided to venture into their own businesses as "Sewing Professionals."

In the '80s, home-sewers went public. Countless numbers of home-sewers turned pro, getting business licenses and all the trappings that go with running a business.

In order to gain recognition as serious sewing professionals, and to support their businesses, women began to unite together in an effort to support one another through networking. Networking was the ideal vehicle for female sewing entrepreneurs to take their goods and services to the market place. When one sewing professional couldn't engage in a project, she simply referred it to another sewing professional. During business hours, they hung up their aprons and turned on their sewing machines.

The '90s found a growing number of women, from all walks of life, entertaining the thought of going into a sewing business, with only the need to know how to go about doing so.

The "Business" Of Sewing is dedicated to those women who insisted on being taken seriously as home-sewing professionals, and to assisting the women of today who desire to join the ranks of their predecessors, as serious sewing professionals.

STUDENTS AND TEACHERS

There have been enormous budget cuts in our educational system. The Home Economics departments that offer sewing classes need quality materials, thus creating a need for them to depend on outside resources.

Students and teachers alike want books with subject matter that speaks to the issues at hand, issues such as how they can start a business without spending an additional two to four years on a business degree, and what it takes to become a professional. The list continues to grow as students become passionate regarding sewing professionally. This book addresses these issues and many more.

CLIENTS

The clients of sewing professionals make their needs clear—they want a garment made of the highest quality materials, they want it to be completed in a timely manner, and they want the service they receive from the sewing professional to be *professional!*

Client interaction and the art of being professional are not part of the sewing curriculum. Consequently, there is an extreme need to educate the sewing professional as well as the student on how to master both.

Clients who engage the services of sewing professionals are both wise and sophisticated. Some however, have experienced such poor service from sewing professionals that it led them to become less trusting when it comes to employing their services. This attitude can be somewhat intimidating to the novice sewing professional. However, it serves to put the sewing profession on notice that clients will not stand for inferior service.

The "Business" Of Sewing illustrates how to employ professional standards and techniques, thus eliminating the possibility of clients receiving inferior service due to lack of professionalism.

ARE YOU REALLY READY?

To answer the question: "How do I know if I'm really ready?" you must first ask yourself the following questions:

✂ Do I have the Desire?

✂ Do I have relentless determination?

✂ Am I willing to acquire and employ sufficient knowledge to make my goals a reality?

✂ Am I willing to stay positive in spite of the temptation to give in to fear and self-doubt?

✂ Do I believe in myself?

If you were able to answer "Yes" to the above questions, CONGRATULATIONS... you are on your way to becoming a successful sewing professional!

BUSINESS VS. HOBBY

If you have not defined your business and are choosing various sewing projects for money, chances are you are running your business as a hobby.

Do you give price quotes according to who the prospective client is? Or, do you have a complete price sheet illustrating what you charge? Have you set standards of operation for your business, or do you only work on projects when you are in the mood? Are you focused when it comes to working and completing a project that has a definite deadline? Do you enjoy working under pressure and meeting deadlines? Or, do you give clients an estimated completion date? Are you easily distracted by internal as well as external interruptions?

What are external and internal interruptions? An internal interruption is one that exists within the confines of one's own business. These interruptions tend to be more controllable. An external interruption is one that exists *outside* the basic control of one's business, and you have less influence on the immediate outcome of such an occurrence. The above questions are just a few that you should consider when deciding to sew as a professional.

Perhaps you are an individual who is extremely passionate about sewing, and you experience a real sense of accomplishment from taking a flat piece of fabric and molding it into the latest fashion silhouette. But, when it comes to sewing for others, you just do not seem to have the same burning desire. This is a sign that you had better stick to sewing as a hobby rather than as a business.

Sewing as a business requires being motivated to complete *each and every project* in a timely manner. Working with deadlines is a <u>must</u>. Clients do not want to hear about your personal problems interfering with the completion of their projects. If you cannot commit your business to paper (in the form of a Business Plan) and institute a plan of action, sewing as a business is definitely not for you. A business has stringent requirements, with great monetary rewards...if properly managed.

SPECIALIST VS. GENERALIST

Some professional sewers support the theory that being a generalist (taking on various types of projects) has its rewards. Others maintain that being a specialist provides the opportunity to target a more defined market.

A number of sewing professionals prefer to work on a variety of different projects, as they feel this enables them to earn more money.

At any rate, you must decide what it is *you* like best, and pursue that course of action. For example, if you find that you especially enjoy working specifically with wedding gowns, bridesmaids, and cocktail attire; you should consider being a specialist in the area of wedding and special occasion attire.

Being a specialist gives you the opportunity to become an expert in one given field. You can focus and narrow your concentration to specific projects.

It has been said that when you specialize in a given field, it is easier to market your goods and services, mainly because you can pinpoint your target market.

Being a specialist allows you to tailor your advertising campaign to a specific audience. Conversely, as a generalist accepting all types of projects (tailoring, alterations, special occasion and wedding, etc.), your advertising cannot be targeted toward a specific clientele.

Meanwhile, there are those who believe that being a specialist limits your opportunity to increase business, due to the narrow market availability. However, specializing increases one's skill level, resources and credibility in the field. Listed on the following page are a few of the various types of markets available to the sewing professional.

SPECIALIST VS. GENERALIST . . . ?

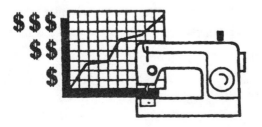

1. Custom Tailoring
2. Weddings/Special Occasion
3. Children's Clothing
4. Home Decor
5. Sewing for the Handicapped
6. Costumes
7. Alterations
8. General Sewing

The preceding list could be defined more specifically. For example, in the field of custom tailoring, you could specialize in women's clothing only. Any one of the above categories could be further defined depending upon your interest and experience.

Before selecting a category, you should take a sheet of paper and list the tasks involved in each. Rate each task according to your desire and ability for that particular task.

If you have difficulty in one area, or lack the proper knowledge, it can be overcome if you have the desire. We will discuss how to increase your skill level in more detail later in the chapter titled *"Do I Have Sufficient Knowledge."*

However, at this point you are trying to establish your specific market through examining your likes and dislikes for specific tasks directly related to each market.

For instance, you may find great pleasure in all the gathering and detailed work that is associated with making little girls' dresses. If this is the case, then children's clothing would certainly be your niche. On the other hand, you may dislike the padstitching, shaping and detailed craftsmanship involved with custom tailoring. This would definitely eliminate custom tailoring as a possibility. It all depends on what tasks you enjoy, as well as the markets in which you possess the greatest knowledge.

Once your area of interest has been identified, this becomes your market. Now you must find the clientele for your market. We will examine how to attract your customer later in the chapter entitled *"Successfully Marketing Your Business."*

The truth of the matter is that whether you choose to become a specialist or a generalist, your ability to gain sufficient clientele to become successful will be partly dependent upon how you market your business. The following example illustrates how valuable marketing is to the success of a business whether you choose to be a specialist or a generalist.

A novice sewing professional, who specialized in the field of children's clothing, invested a great deal of time and money; only to learn the value of marketing the hard way. The client phoned me and was very upset, feeling that her business was failing. We set an appointment for consultation, and after hearing her concerns regarding not having sufficient clientele to support her business, I began to inquire as to her efforts to market her business.

She replied by saying, "I didn't think the use of marketing techniques was important. When I decided to start my business I did so because my neighbors, friends and family always utilized my services."

She was an excellent seamstress, and consistently received high praise for her work. As a result of receiving such high praise from those individuals regarding her work, she felt that they alone would provide her with enough work to support her business.

It is clear to see she did not do her homework. By doing so she would have discovered that a business cannot rely solely on neighbors, friends and family. The failure of her business was directly related to the fact that she neglected to see the need to market her new business.

I gently pointed out that it is great to have those individuals as clients, however, it simply is not enough to sustain a business, and that marketing her business would have greatly increased her potential for success.

After developing a marketing plan which resulted in an 80% increase in revenue within the first quarter of implementation, she is quick to tell anyone that marketing *does* pay off!

It is imperative that you advertise and promote your business. You must inform the public that you are available; and you must educate them on the type of goods and services you have to offer, be it specialized or general.

To educate your clients of your services, the use of a detailed Business Policy is an excellent resource. See example below.

BUSINESS POLICY©

I take great pride in working with all of my clients. It is my policy to complete each and every project on time without sacrificing quality.

To accomplish this goal, I have established certain criteria that I follow. *Clients are scheduled by appointment only*, this insures that no client will be inconvenienced by waiting.

I schedule only those projects that can be successfully completed in a given time period, this practice guarantees that all deadlines are met.

Clients are asked to *call ahead to cancel appointments*. Missed appointments, without notification, are subject to a charge of $10.00.

An extensive number of patterns, notions, and fabrics, are available to accommodate special order request. All notions, patterns and fabric will be billed directly to the client. Quality and client satisfaction is my main concern. I welcome those clients who wish to provide their own notions and fabric, however, I reserve the right to refuse to work with fabric of inferior quality.

All consultations are billed at the rate of $19.00 per hour. If you elect to employ my services to construct your garment/s, the first hours consultation fee will be waived and applied to your bill. Subsequent consultation hour/s will be billed at the normal rate and therefore will not be credited to your bill.

All consultation fees are due at the time of consultation. A 50% deposit on labor is also due at that time. Special purchases for notions and fabric require the actual amount, or an estimated amount due at the time you sign the Consultation/Work agreement herein known as the contract. Any money left over as a result of a special purchase will be credited to the clients account.

All charges for labor, notions, fabric, etc., will be discussed with the client in detail prior to acceptance of the contract.

Prior to signing the contract, *clients are encouraged to read the Business Policy, and ask any questions they have regarding policies and procedures.* You will be asked to initial the section of the contract entitled "Business Policy Received", thus confirming that you have been given a copy of the Business Policy and have a thorough understanding of its contents.

2 Do You Have Sufficient Knowledge?

Having the ability to assess your knowledge and skill level is very important to the quality of work you will produce for your clients. Sewing as a profession requires that you set and meet standards of quality and production. After all, clients are paying you for your knowledge and expertise; therefore you are expected to stay current in your field.

Take inventory of your knowledge and skill level by making a list of questions. Listed below are just a few to stimulate your thought process.

○ Are you familiar with the latest technological advances in your field?

○ Is your skill level equal to or better than commercial standards?

○ Are there any construction techniques you feel deficient in?

O Can you draft a pattern from a sketch or a picture?

O Do you know the various figure types and the appropriate styles for each?

O Complete the list with your own questions

CRITIQUING YOUR WORK

There are a number of ways to critique your work. Having your work critiqued by someone else will help you to gain an understanding of where you stand with respect to your knowledge and skill level. To initiate a personal assessment, you might consider visiting one of the major department stores that carry designer clothing. In reviewing the various garments, determine if you have the skills needed to complete the garments. Are you up-to-date with the latest methods of construction utilized?

Another way to evaluate your skills is to contact a fashion design school and employ the wisdom of an instructor. Teachers take tremendous pride in helping to increase the knowledge and skill level of those who take their sewing seriously. You will find that some instructors are very happy to assist you, provided they have the time, and will share valuable knowledge and wisdom. They can often suggest ways for you to brush up on your sewing skills. To receive the full benefit of their knowledge and wisdom, you should enroll in one of the leading fashion merchandising courses offered at your local college or university.

If you have the opportunity, visit one of the design schools' libraries. You would be amazed at the various magazines and leaflets packed with wonderful information regarding sewing trends and techniques.

Have you ever considered having your work critiqued by a tailor? Enlist the comments of an expert tailor. Tailors exude pride in their work. For centuries tailors have been thought of as highly skilled and well respected. European tailors, English to be exact, have always been held in the highest regard. One benefit that will result from getting an appraisal from a tailor is that generally they will share trade secrets with you. This is not to suggest that all will do so; however, they tend to be extremely passionate about their work. Frequently they will go into great detail to illustrate a point, which, no doubt, will be to your benefit.

If you belong to a network organization, here is a good place to get some advice. Have a group of your peers critique your work. If you choose this method, be sure that those who critique your work are indeed experts in the field that you specialize in. Any one of these methods may yield the desired results. However, you must take care to insure that the individuals you select are qualified to give you advice. Remember—before accepting advice from anyone, you must take inventory of *their* qualifications.

CONTINUING EDUCATION

Change is inevitable—it does not limit itself to any one particular profession. In order to stay abreast of the current changes in your profession, you must constantly strive to increase your knowledge. There are a number of ways to accomplish this, listed below are just a few.

Books/Tapes

One of the best ways to update your knowledge and skills is through reading books. Books allow you the opportunity to review subject matter as often as you like. The library is an excellent resource for books on sewing.

A complete listing of published books on sewing and sewing related topics can be found in *Books In Print*, published by the R.R. Bowker Company, P.O. Box 1807, Ann Arbor, MI 48106.

Books In Print lists current books by subject, title, and author. It is printed annually, and has updates periodically throughout the year. *Books In Print* can be found in the reference section of your local library and can not be checked out. The reference librarian or information assistant will be happy to help you locate and secure information.

Another resource you may find helpful is *Paperbound Books in Print*, also published by the R.R. Bowker Company. It lists books currently available by subject, title, and author. A complete listing of publishers' addresses are given, affording you the opportunity to write requesting a listing of additional books on sewing.

Through modern technology the VCR was born—a marvelous tool which opened new avenues for increasing knowledge. One of the nicest features of being able to view videos is that you can see what is taking place, and you have the capability to repeat steps that you missed or were somewhat unclear about.

This text will have a companion video also entitled *The "Business" Of Sewing*. To obtain information regarding the various sewing products available by Collins Publications send a legal-sized, self-addressed, stamped envelope to:

Collins Publications
Customer Service
3233 Grand Avenue Suite N-294
Chino Hills, CA 91709

There are a number of excellent videos available to the sewing professional. Nancy Zieman is a celebrated sewing professional who has expertise in many fields: Custom Tailoring, Home Decor, Quilting, Crafts, Costumes, Special Occasion, Wedding, and much more. She is the host of a cable television program entitled *"Sewing With Nancy"*, where she discusses how to master various sewing techniques. You may view her programs by checking your local listings under cable television. In addition , she has a video club which features a host of sewing professionals in all fields who have de-

tailed video tapes available. She also has a catalog,
entitled *"Nancy's Notions"* where you may purchase books, hard-to-find notions and a bevy of
excellent sewing-related items. *Nancy's Notions* also
has special discounts for teachers and professionals in the industry. You may reach *Nancy's Notions*
toll-free at 800-833-0690.

An important resource for books, videos and
notions is *Clotilde Inc.*, 1909 S.W. First Ave., Fort
Lauderdale, FL 33315, phone 305-761-8655.

Another excellent resource is *"Fit For You."*
They offer a vast array of unique and hard-to-find
notions, as well as an ample assortment of patterns.
They feature an extensive list of popular books
guaranteed to be helpful to the novice as well as the
seasoned professional. They also stock and carry
numerous videos, which can either be purchased
or rented. To receive a catalog on notions or videos,
or to obtain information regarding various products available, send a legal size, self-addressed
stamped envelope to:

FIT FOR YOU
781 Golden Prados Drive
Diamond Bar, CA 91765

Noted sewing authority Shirley Adams has a
cable television program called *"The Sewing Connection."* She also has a series of books and video
tapes available.

To receive more information, you may contact her at:

The Sewing Connection
922 Cheltenham Way
Plainfield, IN 46168

Fairchild Books takes the spotlight for providing excellent resources to home-sewers/sewing professionals, major fashion institutes, college and universities specializing in the field of fashion sewing, design, and draping; pattern drafting, tailoring and alterations, as well as fitting and grading techniques. To obtain more information, contact them at:

Fairchild Books, Marketing Dept.
7 West 34th St.
New York, NY 10001
Phone 800-247-6622

Robbie Fanning, of Open Chain Publishing Co., offers a variety of books in various different sewing fields. In addition to books, she also has a newsletter entitled "The Creative Machine" (it's so full of good information, it should be classified as a small book). To obtain a catalog, or to subscribe to the newsletter, you may write to:

Open Chain Publishing Co.
P.O. Box 2634-NL
Menlo Park, CA 94026

If you need hands-on training, continuing education classes held at adult education facilities are ideal. Call your local high school or community college. They generally offer a variety of classes in all types of subjects.

A cost-effective method of continuing education may be offered through your community. Check with your local Chamber of Commerce for a full listing of community-held classes. If you need substantial training in a specific area, your best alternative would be to enroll in one of the colleges or trade schools offering specialized courses geared toward your specific needs.

MAGAZINES

For years, pattern magazines have been offering valuable information to sewing professionals. Articles on sewing techniques, up-to-date notions, trends in textile, the latest in modern equipment, as well as current fashion designs by noted fashion designers; can be found in sewing magazines. A complete listing of excellent magazines appears in the *Resource Guide* of this text. However there are several magazines I feel address the needs of a vast array of sewing professionals, and they are: Sew News, McCall's, Butterick, Vogue and Threads. A subscription to any of these magazines would be well worth the investment.

PATTERN COMPANIES

The leading pattern companies invest in continuing education for their consumers. They offer a number of helpful books, pamphlets, video tapes and much more. You may write to them for more information. Following are the address of the major pattern companies:

McCall's Pattern Co.
1110 Penn Plaza
New York, NY 10001

Simplicity Pattern Co.
200 Madison Ave., 5th Floor
New York, NY 10016

(Note: **Simplicity** also carries **New Look** and **Style** patterns)

Butterick/Vogue
161 Avenue of the Americas
New York, NY 10013

Burda Patterns
P.O. Box 670628
Marietta, GA 30066

NETWORK AND PROFESSIONAL ORGANIZATIONS

Networking

Networking is a powerful use of human resources. Networking can offer stability and support to professional women. Men have been networking for years, and realize the value in the so called "Old Boy" network.

Many rewarding business endeavors are formulated over network meetings. Being a part of such organizations can cut through unnecessary red tape. Networking with other professionals can also increase your profit margin through lowering overhead expenses.

This is not to suggest that you should start network groups at the expense of joining other professional organizations. However, it will provide you with immediate results that can be realized through small network groups.

What are some of the benefits? The most important benefits are building a support system of a group of your peers, sharing valuable information in your trade or field of specialty, increasing business through referrals, and saving on notions and supplies through buying in bulk.

It is relatively easy to organize a small network group. You only need to assemble sewing professionals who have the same interests as yourself. You can start by issuing a letter stating the purpose of the network organization, and by setting up the first meeting to outline your goals and purpose.

If your main purpose is to save overhead through buying supplies in bulk, there are a few guidelines you need to follow. First, establish a list of notions and supplies needed. Contact the various suppliers, who can be found in the Business-to-Business Phone Directory. Draft a letter asking them the following:

- What are their minimum opening orders? Dollar? Quantity?

- What are their credit terms?

- Do they offer extra discounts?

- Do they have a local sales representative?

- Do they have samples or a catalog?

By a number of you pooling your resources together to order in volume, you qualify to receive large discounts. Manufacturers respect volume buying and give generously to those who demonstrate the ability to function in that capacity. You must have a Sellers Permit in order to buy from wholesale suppliers. One such supplier is Lions Notions. They are distributors for some of the major notions manufacturers such as: Talon, Dritz, Pellon, Rowenta, Schmetz, Gingher's, Offray, and many more.

To obtain more information, you may contact them at:

Lions Notions Inc.
1260 North Lakeview Ave.
Anaheim, CA 92807
Phone 800-222-0288

PROFESSIONAL ORGANIZATIONS

PACC

Being a member of a professional organization offers a myriad of benefits to the sewing professional. One such organization is the PACC.

PACC is an acronym for the Professional Association Of Custom Clothiers, and is an organization dedicated to the novice as well as the seasoned sewing professional.

PACC'S co-founder and chairperson, noted author, instructor and owner of her own custom tailoring business, Kathleen Spike clearly stated the goals and objectives of the organization in a recent newsletter to its members: "One of the main goals is to work to elevate your professional visibility and status in the eyes of the public both locally and nationally. As a result, in years to come the public will have been taught how to hire you and how to fairly pay you. Yes, I think it is a goal we can achieve."

She goes on to say, "Our membership will include not only established sewing professionals (formal membership), but also those who are in the developmental stages or are investigating sewing as a business (intern membership). It's important to me that we extend a hand to budding business women. It is the perfect environment for them to begin to learn, grow, and to make correct business and technical decisions."

Over the past year, I have had the pleasure of getting to know Kathleen Spike, and she genuinely cares about the progress of her fellow sewing professionals.

Whether you are a "budding" business woman or a well-seasoned sewing professional, don't pass up the opportunity to belong to such a worthwhile organization as PACC. For further information you may write to:

**Professional Association Of
Custom Clothiers (PACC)**
1375 Broadway, 4th Floor
New York, NY 10018

American Sewing Guild

The American Sewing Guild is a national organization with local chapters. These chapters have general meetings as well as neighborhood groups.

They offer newsletters, special events such as fashion shows and educational seminars featuring noted sewing authorities. They are a wonderful source of support for their members. For membership or to get more information regarding a chapter nearest you write to:

Jean Fristensky
National Director
P.O. Box 8476
Medford, OR 97504-0476

SewCiety

SewCiety offers a bevy of excellent resources for the novice and the seasoned sewing professional. Membership includes: *SewCiety Pages*—a quarterly newsletter featuring fashion forecast, how-to tips, new serger and sewing techniques, and much more; and *SewCiety Video Newsletter*—a 45-minute video featuring the latest garment construction, sewing notions and accessories. Other benefits include a portfolio; *SewCiety Extras*—a supplement to the *SewCiety Pages*; notions samples; as well as a SewCiety collectors pin, membership card and certificate. To join, contact:

E. Ann Riegel
SewCiety
c/o Baby Lock U.S.A.
P.O. Box 730
Fenton, MO 63026-0730

3 Starting Your Business

GOALS

In almost every text regarding goal setting, they will advise you to: (1) Set your goals, and (2) Make realistic and attainable goals.

One could argue the validity of whether or not a goal is realistic, or for that matter even attainable. The true test rest on the shoulders of the individual setting the goal. Your ability to analyze the components of goal setting will make a marketable difference in how you accomplish your goal, and there is definitely no contest to the theory that you should set goals. However, you should understand the purpose of goals. Before discussing the purpose of setting goals, we shall examine the types of goals. There are basically two categories of goals:

1. Long-term goals
2. Short-term goals (Interim Goals)

A long-term goal tends to be more global in nature. It is the composition of interim or short-term goals. In other words, a long-term goal is where you want to go...your destination; and the short-term goal is the road map to take you there.

Example: Your long-term goal for the year is to earn $30,000 in your new custom tailoring business. In order to accomplish your long-term goal, a succession of short-term goals must be met. These goals would include obtaining: (1) Licenses and permits, (2) Start-up capital, (3) Equipment and supplies, (4) Advertising to attract clients; and so on. Understanding the types of goals will help you to formulate your long-term and short-term goals. Start with your purpose, which will be the reason you desire to start your business. List your real motivations on paper. This will help you in structuring a plan of attack.

Let's say that you have children, and wish to be available for them. Having a home-based sewing business provides you the opportunity to do so. Your desire to be available for your children will be the main motivation you need in order to start your business.

Everyone who is in business is motivated by some desire. Whether it be wealth, recognition, family, self-accomplishment, love of one's profession, or just the need to be in control of one's life. No matter what your desire, we are all motivated by *something*.

It is clear to see that what could be unrealistic

for some, could be a natural progression for those who possess the knowledge, skill, motivation and desire.

Now that you have your main goal identified, you must draft a *Business Plan*.

BUSINESS PLAN

What is a business plan? A business plan is a guide or outline of how you plan to start your business. The business plan takes you step-by-step through the short-term goals needed to accomplish your long-term goals.

A home-based sewing business will operate more efficiently if you take the time to initiate a business plan. Often small home-based entrepreneurs feel that because they are small there is no need to go through a detailed business plan. Insufficient planning can cause failure, whether the business is large or small.

Chapter One (Knowing When You Are Ready) was a basis for psychologically preparing yourself for the challenges that are involved in operating a business. In addition, you were able to determine your field of concentration, Home Decor, Custom Tailoring, etc. Now you are prepared to get started; and the best way is with a business plan.

Start by listing your goals. Keep your goals firmly planted in your mind. It has been said by many business consultants that you are not serious until you commit to paper.

Writing out the steps that you plan to take to

get your business started is a true test of your commitment to accomplish your goal. Let's examine the components of a business plan. NOTE: While it is important to follow a business plan, you must allow some degree of flexibility due to economic and seasonal changes. For example, the third quarter (July, August, September) are traditionally slow for retail clothing stores due to summer vacations. It is advisable that you research to determine any seasonal trends in your business.

COMPONENTS OF A BUSINESS PLAN

Basic Elements
☐ List your goals (Purpose)
☐ State the nature of your business
☐ Determine the legal form of business
 (Sole Proprietor, Partnership,etc.)
☐ Select a name (Research Name)
☐ Define days/hours of operation
☐ Check requirements for: Permits, License,
 Zoning
☐ Select a tentative Start Date

Location/Equipment/Supplies
☐ Describe layout/design for: (1) Office
 (2) Sewing Studio
☐ List forms needed for both
☐ Design letterhead and business cards
☐ List equipment needed and on hand for:
 (1) Office (2) Sewing Studio

❑ List notions/other sewing related items
needed for operation

Financial Plan
❑ How much start-up capital will you
need, and how will you obtain the funds?
❑ Establish your pricing policy (See Chapter 5)
❑ Make sales projections
❑ Make a Balance Sheet and Income Statement
❑ Make Cash Flow Projections
❑ Check on insurance
❑ Develop a recordkeeping system
(See Chapter 6)
❑ Formulate an inventory plan
❑ Allow for taxes, subscriptions, continuing
education, etc.
❑ Open a business bank account
❑ List future expansion plans, if any
(See Chapter 8)
❑ Develop a Marketing Plan (See Chapter 7)
❑ Identify your customer
❑ Analyze your competition
❑ Determine what services you will offer
❑ Determine type of advertising/promotions
❑ Establish a budget for advertising/
promotions
❑ Develop an on-going market research plan

Human Resources

❏ Will you hire employees? (See Chapter 8)
❏ Will you utilize subcontractors?
  (See Chapter 8)
❏ Get advice from the following:
  Business Banking Officer, Accountant,
  Insurance Agent, Attorney
❏ Join professional organizations
❏ Contact SBA (Small Business
  Administration) for appointment
  with a SCORE counselor
  (See Resource Guide)

MANAGING YOUR BUSINESS PLAN

A good way to manage your business plan is to purchase 3 X 5 inch index cards, a file box, three section dividers, and three sets of date dividers. Mark your file box "Business plan." Take the three section dividers and label them (1) "Research," (2) "Obtain," and (3) "Completed." Put a set of date dividers behind each section divider and place them in the file box.

The 3 X 5 cards will serve as an excellent tool for writing information regarding each item on your Business Plan. Start at the beginning of your Business Plan and make a 3 X 5 card for every item on your Plan. In the upper right-hand corner, assign a category ("Research," " Obtain," or "Completed") using a different color code for each category. Assign a date the action is to take place and file each card according to its category and date. For cards marked "Research" and "Obtain," mark the dates in your Daily Planner (appointment book). Check your card file daily to keep control of your business plan. When you complete an item under the above categories you simply mark it as completed, and file it under the section titled "Completed." For example, under the section "Basic Elements," the first item is "List Goals." You would: (1) Take your index card and write "List Goals," (2) Write your goals on the card, (3) write on the upper right-hand corner "Completed" in the color code of your choice, and (4) File the card in the Business Plan box under the heading "Completed."

When you have completed all the tasks related to each item, take the completed cards and match them to each item on your Business Plan. If you find that an item requires future follow-up, simply prepare an additional section divider and (1) Date the divider, then (2) mark it "Follow-Up" and place it in the front of the file. This system of managing your Business Plan offers you a way of cross-checking items on your Business Plan to insure that you do not forget to complete a task.

Now that you have gone through all of the steps, you are ready to write your own Business Plan. You simply take the information from your completed cards and write your results on paper, using *Components of A Business Plan* as a guide.

In Chapter 4, we will discuss various topics in each section of the Business Plan. Others will be discussed in detail in the chapters to follow.

4 | What Will You Need?

BASIC ELEMENTS

In this section you will write out your goals, both long and short-term. You will describe the type of business you have selected.

Legal Form of Business

You must decide whether you will operate your business exclusively (as a Sole Proprietor) or if you will elect to have a partner (a Partnership) or form a Corporation.

The easiest form of business is the Sole Proprietorship. A partnership requires two or more individuals to form and can be complicated depending upon the terms of the partnership. If you decide to form a partnership, you must keep in mind that you will have to share major decision making with your partner(s), not to mention other legal complexities.

A Corporation is a legal form of business separate from the individuals who own it. Because of the many advantages and disadvantages involved in forming both the Partnership and the Corporation, it is advisable to seek the advice of a qualified attorney.

Most home-based sewing businesses are operated as Sole Proprietorships. You get to enjoy all the profits, make all the management decisions, and take all the risk. However, you must take precautionary measures to protect yourself through insurance. It wouldn't hurt to consult with an attorney just to have a good understanding of what your liability would be as a sole proprietor.

Selecting a Name

Selecting a name for your business is fun. If you choose a name other than your own, you will have to file what is known as a "DBA" (Doing Business As), also known as a Fictitious Business Statement.

Examples:
Fashions Unlimited Custom Tailoring
Tiffany's Home Decor
Barbie's Clothing

If you select your own personal legal name, you will not need to file a DBA. For example, let's say that your name is Mattie Benton, and you decide to call your business "MATTIE BENTON'S TAILORING." Then, you would not need to file a DBA.

How do I file a DBA?

You must first obtain your Business License, then you must register your fictitious business name by filing it with the city or county in which you will conduct your business. You will have to place an ad in a local newspaper. It should run for four consecutive issues. This will serve to notify the public of the legal owner of the fictitious business.

Once the ad has been run, you will need to get a Publication Certificate filed with the county or city clerk. Some newspapers will provide the service for you. However, it is your sole responsibility to see that it gets done. If you elect to utilize the newspaper's service, you should get proof that it was indeed done.

NOTE: Every five years you are required to renew your DBA. You are generally notified, however you are expected to see that it gets done regardless. The good news is that you don't have to publish the ad, but you will have to pay a fee to the city or county clerk.

By registering your DBA, you also protect your fictitious business name and give yourself exclusive rights to that name!

Days and Hours of Business

You must give serious consideration to the amount of time you plan to devote to your business. This is very important if you have young children. Will you want to receive clients during the hours that your youngsters are home? Or, will you

mind if your dinner hour is interrupted because a
client can only come after work? What about your
weekends? Will this be a gross imposition on family
time together?

If you plan to operate your business out of your
home you should enlist the feelings of other family
members prior to finalizing your official business
days and hours. You want harmony in your home—
by considering the needs of yourself and your family,
you will accomplish this goal.

PERMITS, LICENSE AND ZONING

Licensing
Call your local city or county clerk to find out
what the requirements are to operate your business. Your Chamber of Commerce is also an excellent source. It is wise to inquire before setting up
your business. There are severe penalties for operating without a license if your city requires that you
have one.

It should be noted that some cities will not
permit a home-based business. If this is the case,
you will want to discover this prior to investing a
great deal of time and money.

If your city will not allow you to operate your
business from your home there are other alternatives. Contact a local cleaners, and negotiate a lease
for a small portion of space. You could also offer
their clients alterations, and give the owner a percentage in lieu of rent. This would only serve to

enhance both businesses. But, be sure the terms are spelled out in a contract. You should prepare the contract and list what your needs are. Leave some flexibility to negotiate terms with the owner, as he or she may have some suggestions that could be helpful for both of you. No matter what happens, don't give up. Think of other alternatives. If you plan to operate out of someone else's business, it is advisable to have your clients utilize your mailing address for correspondence. You may want all your business mail to come to your home.

There are cities that do not require a license but issue what is called a Home Use Permit. They have specific requirements as well. Check to see that you meet those requirements first.

Additional Permits

Other permits might be needed. There are other agencies that control the use of your home for business. Consult your local city or county clerk, or the Chamber of Commerce. The most common ones are the police, fire and health departments; you may need permits from these departments.

Seller's Permit

A Sellers Permit is also referred to as Resale Number or Resale Certificate. Contact your State Board of Equalization for information regarding rules for application. Some states require you to apply in person, others will process your application by mail.

Not all businesses require the use of a Seller's Permit. If you do business in a state that collects sales tax, and you engage in the sale of taxable goods and services, then you will need a permit. For example, if you purchase items that are subject to tax (fabric, zippers, thread) and sell them to your clients (whole or in part), you need a Resale Permit.

Requirements on the collection of taxes vary from business to business. A thorough understanding of the rules and regulations governing sellers permits and taxes is a must. Your State Board of Equalization has information regarding when to collect taxes for all types of businesses, so be sure to request sales tax information.

There are some advantages to having a permit—it allows you to purchase fabric, notions and other items at wholesale prices, which generally results in a discount. This gives you an increased profit margin. When you purchase wholesale, you do not pay the taxes. However, you are expected to collect the taxes from the end users...your clients. Please note that all purchases made with your Resale Permit *must* be for resale in your business. There are stiff penalties for misuse of your permit.

Many wholesalers require you to fill out a Resale Card, which is kept on file to verify that you have a resale permit.

The taxes that you collect from your clients must be reported and submitted to the State Board either quarterly or annually. The board will inform you of your reporting period at the time they issue your permit.

A "State, Local and District Sales and Use Tax Return" form is sent to all those required to submit taxes. If you do not receive this form prior to your reporting deadline, it is your responsibility to obtain the form and meet the reporting deadline.

The State Board of Equalization offers classes periodically to assist you in filling out the form, as well as to inform you of tax laws. They are eager to help—all it takes is a phone call.

Zoning

There are zoning regulations that vary from city to city. Consequently, you need to know what they are and whether or not they affect your business.

These issues are generally governed by the Building Inspector or the Planning Department. Some cities have special Zoning Administration that control zoning. In addition, if you reside in a housing development that abides by a Homeowner's Association, you should inquire as to whether the covenants preclude you from operating your business. Listed below are some questions you should ask regarding zoning regulations:

1. What are the zoning ordinances for your city or county?
2. How is your property zoned?
3. What is allowed in your zone?

What should you do if you aren't zoned for operating a home-based business? There are some options available. You could contact other businesses to see if they would allow you to place your license there. As was stated previously, if you choose this option be sure to have your mail come to your home or obtain a post office box. As a last resort, you could rent a small office suite.

If you decide that you would not be happy with the above alternatives, you might consider applying for a Use Permit. This would allow you to operate your business from your home even though it isn't zoned for it. The permit would have to be approved by the department that governs zoning. Or, you could apply for a Variance. This is when you actually ask the local zoning board to waive their restrictions. Be prepared to prove that your business will not cause any significant inconvenience to the neighborhood, such as parking problems, noise, pollution, etc.

As a final option, you could work to get the zoning ordinance changed through an amendment. If you could get enough people interested, you might be able to effect a change.

Start Date

Through all of your planning, you will need to have a start date in mind. The start date will be the formal date you plan to start your business. When you select a start date make sure it is one that is comfortable for you.

NOTE: Keep a record of all the costs involved as you work through each section of your business plan, as this information is very valuable in determining start-up costs.

Location, Equipment, and Supplies

Planning your work space can be a rewarding experience. When you develop your plan for your sewing room or space, make sure it is an environment that you feel good in. It should be functional and visually pleasing. Placement of equipment and supplies should be relatively handy. Being well organized can speed up production and bring you great pleasure while working. An excellent way to get started is to gather pencils, pens, grid paper, tape, ruler, protractor and a see through template with a variety of shapes. You will use the grid paper and the rest of the supplies you gathered to map out the design of the room and placement of equipment and supplies.

Make a list of the equipment that you will need and divide the list in half. On one side you will list equipment you have on hand, on the opposite side you will list equipment you need to obtain. Repeat the same process for your supplies.

From the above list you will draft the layout and design of your sewing room and office. If you are combining your office and sewing area, you will only need one layout and design plan. When you are developing your layout, think of the flow of work. For example, you would place your sewing

machine close to your serger for convenience. Your
pressing tools should be placed nearby so that you
can move from garment construction to pressing
with minimal of effort.

Another crucial area of consideration is your
cutting space. There are a number of options to
choose from. If you have the space for a 30" X 60"
cutting area, there are a couple of ways you can set
up a cutting area very inexpensively.

The first way is to purchase (4) saw-horse brackets, a sheet of plywood 30" x 60" and approximately
1/2" to 3/4" thick, enough 2' x 4's to make the legs
and cross bars, a 30" x 60" rotary cutting mat (optional), and some paint. Have (8) 2' x 4's cut to the
height that would be comfortable for you to work,
and (2) more cut 29" inches each for the cross bars.
Insert the (8) 2' x 4's into the saw horse brackets
vertically and take (2) saw horse brackets and place
a 2 'x 4' horizontally. Repeat for the remaining two.
Now you have created two supporting units to rest
your 30" x 60" inch plywood tabletop on. Place the
two units a sufficient distance apart to balance the
top. At this point you may want to apply a coat of
paint to the legs and sides of the table top to make
it more attractive. Make sure that all exposed wood
surfaces are sanded smooth. If you like, you could
also apply some lace trim to cover the metal saw-
horse brackets. Then, apply your rotary mat—and
you are ready to go! A large cutting area at the
proper height will help to preserve your back; the
cutting height should be high enough to take the

strain off your back. You will not need a rotary cutting mat if you won't be using a rotary cutter.

The second way is to purchase a pattern file cabinet from a fabric store, a piece of plywood 30" x 60" and a rotary cutting mat (optional). If you can't find a fabric store that has one for sale at the time, you may substitute by using a wooden cabinet with drawers. The cabinet serves two purposes: one, to balance the table top; and two, to store patterns, fabrics and notions.

I store my patterns numerically. I use file dividers, the file dividers are labeled starting at 1000 to 9000. For example, pattern number 7896 would be placed behind the divider labeled 7000.

When I purchase a pattern. I catalog it for inventory purposes. Then, depending upon what I will use it for, I may take the contents out and store in a large Ziploc freezer bag with the illustration side face up. I then place the pattern envelope in a plastic protector sheet to be filed in my pattern notebook. It will be filed under Suit, Dress, Pants, Blouse, Combination, Leisure/Activewear, Outerwear, or Lingerie.

Getting and staying organized is a *must*. Productivity is greatly enhanced when you are organized. To help achieve your goal, you should consider how you plan to store your fabric and sewing supplies. Here are some ways to help you organize.

I love beautiful boxes, and I found that I had a collection of silver boxes in all shapes and sizes from Nordstrom department stores. I labeled them, and I use them to store my notions. The boxes are placed on shelves in my sewing studio and look very attractive. I can readily find items needed at a glance.

For small items of quantity, such as buttons, I colorize them and place them in small plastic bags to be stored in my silver boxes. I use a large number of black, white, browns, cream, neutral and derivations thereof, so I file them together for easy access.

Plastic shoe boxes work well for storing notions and can be stacked neatly on shelves. Since you can see the contents, you may prefer not labeling them.

On the wall above my workstation that houses my machines, I have a magnetic bar that holds all of my cutting tools, bodkins, tracing wheels, etc. It is very handy—I don't have to stop and search for notions. Above that bar I have covered a large rectangular piece of peg board, onto which I use to place pattern guide sheets, notes and anything of interest.

To house some of my thread, I purchased several June Tailor thread racks. I covered each with lace and lavender ribbon so that it matches the decor of the rest of my studio.

For a pleasing effect, I chose a soft, yellow, floral-printed chintz fabric with white lace and lavender ribbon. I made my valances, covered my chair, bulletin board and one waste basket. The color of my carpet is a rich, seafoam green. The seafoam green is carried throughout the fabric's floral pattern, with a hint of lavender and baby pink. The combination gives a happy, springtime effect; which is pleasing to the eye, and makes for a comfortable work environment.

When planning the layout and design of the sewing studio my first consideration was for production and organization. I chose an L-shaped layout for my workstation. It complements the room and provides maximum utility. I started by planning to have a ceiling-to-floor cabinet for storage. After consulting with a contractor, it was suggested that I reconsider having the cabinet go to the ceiling. I am pleased that I followed his suggestion—I have a place to showcase the most recent pattern catalog and my green plants, which add so much life to a room. I use the cabinet to store large quantities of shoulder pads and zippers, serger thread (which is keep in plastic containers by color), and many other supplies.

The L-shaped workstation starts from the side of the cabinet and continues on around. I use shelving on two main walls above the workstation. It helps to keep all of my notions at my fingertips, and to house the many books and magazines, current client files, forms, and teaching supplies that I have.

On my workstation, I have three sewing machines and two sergers and a small pressing area. In the corner space, I have my Elna Steam Press, and directly below it (in stackable bins) I have my lining fabrics. Since they are stored in the corner space underneath my workstation, it does not hamper my ability to move from one machine to the other. At the end of the workstation I have a small file cabinet in which I store small yardage of interfacing. One drawer is labeled "Sew-in" and the other "Fusible." On top of the file cabinet, I keep my portable speaker phone, answering machine and a radio. I enjoy soft music as I work and my clients tend to appreciate it as well. However,I never listen to music when teaching—it tends to distract the students.

On the entry wall is a full length mirror. On the wall next to it I place my license and a poster explaining my services, and on that same wall, neatly arranged, is a full line of current pattern catalogs. I find that clients really enjoy having access to current pattern catalogs. I give the client a Request Form to make it easy when selecting patterns from the various catalogs. The Request Form will be covered in Chapter Three.

In the closet I store huge amounts of fabric and interfacing; some I keep on hangers and others are neatly folded. The interfacing that I purchase in large quantity I keep on the bolts. My cutting area is close to my closet for easy access, leaving ample walking space on all sides for laying out and cutting projects.

Visual appearance is very important. On the closet doors are neatly arranged pictures of current fashions. To the left is a small gold hook for displaying my latest fashion creation or a clients' project.

The south wall is dedicated to capturing client interest. There are three gold hooks on which I place fashions either by color or category. Directly above,

I display pictures of current fashions by leading designers.

I belong to several fabric clubs, and I utilize the remainder of the wall to showcase fabric swatch cards. In the middle of the wall are swatches of Ultrasuede, Ultraleather and Facile, in just about every color imaginable. These swatches are categorized and placed on silver rings.

Swatch cards that can't be placed on the wall are neatly arranged on the floor below. When I receive a new fabric swatch card, I retire the older one to spotlight the new. There is something magical about seeing color and texture that excites clients. They can't resist buying, which is great because it keeps you with repeat business!

Whether you are working with a small space or a large room, you must plan your work area. Here are two resources I feel would be helpful. You may call to order:

1. "Organize Your Sewing Area"
   Nancy's Notions, 800-833-0690
   (Ask for the video and transcript)

2. "Trends In Sewing Room Design"
   Palmer/Pletsch, 503-274-0687
   (Ask for *Bulletin No.1*)

If you are going to utilize separate areas for your office and your sewing studio, you will need to draft separate layout and design plans for each.

Consider what activities will take place in the office. Will you conduct business with your clients there, or just utilize the office for clerical and recordkeeping functions? Follow the steps mentioned above for the layout and design of your office. Start by listing supplies and equipment needed and those on hand.

My office is a separate room from my sewing studio. Since I greet clients in my office, I chose a layout and design to accommodate client interaction as well as clerical and recordkeeping activities.

In the office, there is a large executive desk complete with customized client chairs and an executive chair (which protects my back during long working hours). I have a matching lateral file and credenza which house a number of client and other business files.

On the north wall is a small bookshelf, laser printer, desk, and a large bookshelf; and on the opposite side of the bookshelf is a complete set of pattern catalogs. I prefer to keep pattern catalogs in both my office and my sewing studio. When a client first comes to me for consultation, it makes it easier to have them on hand in the office as well.

On the south wall is my credenza and lateral file. I use the credenza to store supplies and small office equipment. Next to the lateral file is a brass plant stand with green ferns.

There is adequate lighting throughout the room. I placed one lamp on the end of the lateral file and another on the end of the credenza. A third light is placed near my desk on top of the small bookshelf.

The phone and answering machine are placed on top of the credenza along with some decorative items to add life to the office.

On top of my desk is my computer monitor, a small desk caddie for items such as pencils, pens, scissors, stamps, stamp pads, etc.; and the tower unit (CPU) rests on the floor near the printer stand. In addition to these items, I have a small file holder to store new client packets and client pick-up files.

All of my decorative pictures were chosen in a musical theme, and are placed throughout to add surface interest (and they make for great conversation pieces).

I am a big fan of Betty Boop—I have Betty Boop memorabilia all over my office. It seems to make my clients comfortable when they see a personal side of me.

Note: When selecting personal items for your office, make sure that they will not distract from the professional image and are used in moderation. This is especially important if you are going to have clients in your office. Your office, like your sewing area, should be functional *and* visually pleasing.

Design Letterhead and Business Cards

Your business cards and stationery say a great deal about you and your business. You want to convey the impression that you are professional, and a good business card and stationery will do wonders for your image.

You want to select a logo that is representative of your business. A logo is a design of an object, person or can be done with words or letters of the alphabet. You may decide to have a graphic artist design one, or you may select clip art from your local printer. If you own a computer and have desktop publishing or graphic arts programs, you can be extremely creative and save money at the same time. This will eliminate hiring a graphic artist and save money at the printers, because you will have camera ready art; not to mention that your logo will be exclusively yours unlike that of clip art from a printer.

If you decide to have someone design your logo, or if you design one yourself, be sure to protect it by registering it with the Copyright or Patent and Trademark Office. Write them to obtain further information:

Copyright Office
Library of Congress
Washington, D.C. 20559

Patent and Trademark Office
U.S. Department of Commerce
Washington, D.C. 20231

When designing your business cards and stationery, you will want to consider making the type as readable as possible. Make sure that the logo is representative of your business. You also want to be sure that the person reading the card can immediately understand what type of business or service you offer. Keep in mind that your business card is a form of advertisement—so get the most out of it without overdoing it.

Computers

Repetitive clerical and recordkeeping tasks can be accomplished with minimal frustration through the use of a computer. I am constantly amazed at the efficiency with which computers handle, store and retrieve data. Files are easier to manage, you can perform mass mailings through your data based software programs, and generate professional looking promotional pieces through the use of desktop publishing software.

If your budget can't squeeze in the purchase of a new computer system, you might consider leasing a system (which is a wonderful tax shelter). You don't need to start out with something fast such as the 486, you can suffice with a 386SX and some excellent software packages.

Software

If you are just getting started with computers, you might consider an integrated software package. *Microsoft Works* is an excellent choice. Included in this software package are several useful applications: (1) Word processing for writing valuable correspondence, (2) A data base to keep track of valuable contacts (an essential feature for mass mailings), (3) A spreadsheet program for tracking the financial needs of the business, and (4) Communications for sending and retrieving information via modem. A modem utilizes a telephone line which is plugged into your computer, making it possible to communicate with other computers. Another excellent software application is *Windows 3.1*. This program takes the stress out of learning computer commands. It's easy, all you do is point to an icon (a graphic picture) and press a button on your mouse (a small device utilized to initiate commands for the program) and depress a button. It's that simple.

If you desire a more powerful program for word processing with some desktop publishing attributes, then *Wordperfect 5.1* for *Windows* is a very good choice.

Desktop publishing allows entrepreneurs the opportunity to produce excellent marketing and sales promotional pieces at a fraction of the cost. You save on printing costs by producing camera-ready copy. Consequently, you eliminate having to pay a printer for typesetting fees. A desktop publishing software program for brochures, promotional pieces and newsletters is a must. One application which is relatively inexpensive is *First Publisher*. It is fun and user friendly—great for the beginner.

For those with more advanced needs, there are programs such as *Aldus PageMaker* and *Corel Draw*. These programs come with a vast assortment of clip art and graphical editing capabilities. You can bring in documents from your integrated software word processing file and redesign them into sensational pieces for advertisements.

If for some reason you have been reluctant to purchase a computer or software, due to feeling overwhelmed with learning the software programs, you can put your fears to rest. There is a company that provides a wonderful collection of video-taped programs designed to get you up and running in no time flat. *LearnKey* has an excellent series of tapes on the leading software programs. For more information you may call or write to:

LearnKey
93 S. Mountain Way Dr., Box F
Orem, UT 84058
800-937-3279

With a growing number of personal computers among sewing professionals, and with the introduction of state-of-the-art sewing machines that interface with computers, more computer software is becoming available.

There are companies who have recognized the need to fill this void in the sewing industry. Annette Schofield, President of *Livingsoft Inc.*, has done just that through her *Dress Shop* software program. This program actually makes patterns through the use of your computer and a printer. You may contact Livingsoft by calling 800-626-1262 or 619-446-6003 or by writing to:

Livingsoft, Inc.
524 West Dolphin Street
Ridgecrest, CA 93555

Another excellent software program due to be released by Collins Publications will allow you to accurately make pattern adjustments through the use of your computer; and it will increase production and decrease errors.

Collins Publications has come through once again in recognizing another void—they are developing an integrated software program specifically for sewing professionals, as well as business forms, on computer disk. For more information you may write to:

Collins Publications
Software Division
3233 Grand Avenue Suite N-294
Chino Hills, CA 91709

Financial Plan

You will have to determine just how much start-up capital you will need. If you are having difficulty in discovering all the start-up costs, you should consider consulting someone in your field or a local trade association. Ask them what type of start-up costs they incurred during their initial start-up phase. Also, be sure to ask what ongoing expenses they have.

When you complete the research of the items on your Business Plan, you should have an idea of just how much money you will need. Where will you obtain the capital?

Generally, home-based sewing businesses don't require enormous amounts of money to get started. However, if you are starting from scratch without the benefit of a sewing machine, etc., you may find that the initial start-up will be somewhat costly.

There are a number of options available. The most obvious would be to simply take funds from your savings. Or, if the initial amount is more than you can spare, you will have to consider borrowing the funds from a lending institution or possibly a relative or friend.

If you decide to borrow from a bank, then your Business Plan will carry a lot of weight. Banks respect an entrepreneur who has a Business Plan. It gives the impression that you have given thought to your business and are well-prepared.

Your Business Plan along with your credit worthiness will be the decisive factors as to whether or not you will obtain the loan. Be sure to interview several lending establishments to discover how receptive they are to home-based businesses. Spend some time developing a relationship with the bank. Your business banking officer can literally save your business, if you spend the time needed to develop a professional relationship. They can suggest ways to help you accomplish your goals that you may not have considered. They are there to help. Why not take advantage of the service? If you are going to seek a loan from a bank, it would be wise to have an accountant prepare your financial statements. You will need the following:

1. Income and Expense Statement
2. Balance Sheet
3. Cash Flow Projections
4. Sales Projections

On the other hand, if you are going to seek a personal loan and not inform the bank that it is for business, you will not need the above forms and chances are, the process will be less involved. At any rate, you will need to develop a good relationship with your banker, and you will need to open a business bank account. Shop around for a bank that respects your business and offers free checking with unlimited check writing.

Also, don't overlook your Credit Union. They are an excellent source of obtaining capital, and chances are, the funds needed can be borrowed at a much lower rate of interest.

Cash Flow Projections

Once you have completed your research, you should have a fairly accurate account of how much you will need to start your business. You should also have a clear understanding of the ongoing expenses involved in the running of your business.

A Cash Flow Projection is nothing more than a

statement of how much money you have coming in (income) and how much you have going out (expenses). If you hire an accountant to help you in the preparation of a Cash Flow Chart, it will be extremely detailed. However, for the purpose of illustration, we will break it down into its simplest form.

A. <u>CASH ON HAND</u>
1. LOANS
2. SAVINGS
3. ALL OTHERS

B. <u>CASH FROM EXPECTED SALES</u> (SALES PROJECTIONS)

C. <u>TOTAL CASH ON HAND</u> (A+B=C)

D. <u>CASH DISBURSEMENTS</u>
1. LOANS
2. EXPENSES (ALL)
3. ALL OTHERS
E. <u>TOTAL DISBURSEMENTS</u>

F. <u>END OF MONTH CASH BALANCE</u> (C-E=F)

You will prepare the above information for each month. The END OF MONTH figure becomes your CASH ON HAND for the following month.

When considering expenses you should group them into two categories, Fixed and Variable. A fixed expense is one that is paid on a regular basis and whose amount is constant. A variable expense is one in which the amount varies. Listed below are some expenses you might consider.

<u>Fixed</u>	<u>Variable</u>
Rent	Telephone/Utilities
Insurance	Supplies/Stationery
Membership Dues	Printing/Postage
Subscriptions	Travel/Entertainment
Salary	Repairs

How can you project your sales? A sales projection is an estimate. The estimate can be made with some degree of accuracy if you research the market. Keep in mind that here is where you will exercise some degree of flexibility, as there is no absolute way to determine future sales. Another consideration is that you do not have a built-in clientele and you will need some time to develop repeat business that you can count on. You may find that as you progress in your business, you will need to revise your projections. You are probably thinking, "If I can't accurately project my sales, how can I determine my cash flow?"

A rule of thumb: Always build into your start-up capital enough money (working capital) to carry you through the initial start-up period. Most business consultants and financial advisers suggest you have at least six months to one year in reserve. It would be safe to say that when you are calculating how much it will take to get you started, this figure should be worked in as well. This rule is especially crucial if you are depending solely on your business for income. If you have a spouse or other income, and will not depend solely on the income from the business, then you may not need to build in such an enormous reserve.

Income and Expense Statements

The Income and Expense Statement is a tool that you use for showing what income you made during a given month or period, and what expenses you had. The difference between the two will determine whether you made a profit or loss for a given period.

The equation for this is:
Income-Expenses=Net Profit/Loss

Balance Sheet

A balance sheet is a listing of your assets (what you own), such as Cash, Accounts Receivable, Land, Inventory, Equipment, Furniture etc.; minus your liabilities (what you owe) such as Accounts Payable, Loans, etc. The difference between the two is your Net Worth or Capital.

The equation for this is:
Assets-Liabilities=Net Worth or Capital

Due to the complexities involved in the various financial statements, it is advisable that you seek the advice of an accountant. This is vitally important if you are planning on obtaining a bank loan!

Insurance

The name of the game is protection. You want to protect your assets and business from any unforeseen liabilities. The best way is through having good insurance policies—a good insurance plan offers you peace of mind.

If you are operating your business out of your home, then you must not overlook liability insurance, which covers bodily injury or property damage. If you are renting, you will need to consider a renters policy. There are also two other types of insurance you need to consider when extending goods or services to the public sector, and they are Professional and Product Liability. Ask your insurance representative for his suggestions regarding your business needs.

Most insurance companies offer additional policies for very little if you have a homeowners policy with them. The additional policy is commonly known as a Rider. Some professional organizations offer group discounts on certain insurance plans. When you contact your representative, be sure to inquire about the following insurance plans: Health, Worker's Compensation (only if you have employees), Automobile, Disability, Income Protection and Business Life. Keep in mind that as your business progresses, so will your insurance needs. Make insurance a *vital* part of your business plan.

Inventory Plan

Most entrepreneurs dread taking inventory, when in fact, substantial inventory records can increase profit. Knowing what is on hand, how much is needed and when it needs to be replaced can save your business.

You want to have enough on hand to service your clientele, thus insuring that you don't lose a sale or decrease production time by having to stop and purchase an item; or by having to purchase that same item at retail when you could have planned to have it in your inventory at wholesale for half the price.

Knowing what you need to successfully operate your business can save you a great deal of money and increase your profit margin. It will prevent you from overstocking items that don't move rapidly and have very little demand; and it will allow you to discontinue items that are obsolete due to modern technology or lack of demand.

Inventory records provide you with the data to stock supplies that are making money for you. First of all, you are aware when items are low; you know by the usage how often you should place reorders. Therefore, you don't tie up valuable working capital in overstocking, and on slow-moving supplies.

If you can view inventory as a built-in profit-protector, you may began to actually enjoy taking inventory.

What is the best way to keep control of your inventory? There are several ways you can track items: (1) By index cards, (2) With notebook paper, and (3) By computer. The main concern is to develop a system that works for you and to be consistent in taking the inventory.

Tracking fabric can be cumbersome, however there is one way that seems to work. When you purchase fabric, clip the corner of the fabric. On a sheet of plain paper glue the swatch, and assign a number above. If you wish, for quick reference you may put the amount of yardage below the swatch. On an index card or computer, record the amount of yardage, width, date of purchase, care instructions and cost. Your numbering system might go as follows: 1 to 100, resume numbering with A1 to A99, and repeat the process using the letters of the alphabet. Place the sheets into plastic protectors and file them in a notebook.

For fabrics that are too delicate to clip, on your sheet of paper draw a small triangle to represent a swatch of fabric and treat it just as you would an actual swatch. If you cut a loosely woven fabric that tends to fray, add a drop of Fray Check on the edges of your swatch. This serves two purposes (1) It provides a test for using Fray Check on your fabric, and (2) It stops the swatch from raveling.

Marketing Plan

Marketing will be discussed in detail in Chapter Seven, however it should be noted that marketing is an important part of a business plan and funds for marketing should be included in your plan as part of your initial and ongoing cost.

Human Resources

It is very difficult to operate a business without utilizing human resources in one way or another. When you seek the advice of professionals such as Accountants, Insurance Representatives, Attorney's, Banking Officers, etc., you are utilizing human resources. These specialists are part of your professional team. Every successful business employs their services.

The other type of human resources that are very valuable are those of fellow members of your professional or trade associations and network groups. We spoke about getting advice and having your work critiqued by your colleagues in chapter two. It is important to belong to these organizations as they can provide invaluable assistance to you and your business. We will examine the importance of hiring employees and subcontractors later in Chapter Eight.

SMALL BUSINESS ADMINISTRATION (SBA)

In the early fifties Congress recognized a need to have small businesses flourish. As a result of that need, formed the U. S. Small Business Administration also known as the SBA.

The SBA offers many benefits to small business owners such as, free counseling, classes, conferences and very helpful literature on all phases of business.

The SBA also gets involved in helping the small business owner obtain capital for their business. Sometime ago the SBA would loan money directly to applicants who had been refused a loan by at least two banks, and met SBA requirements. Today, however, it is not a common practice for the SBA to loan direct funds to applicants. The SBA makes the banks position secure so that they may lend the funds to the applicants providing they meet certain requirements. Those requirements are (1) credit worthiness (2) you must be able to operate your business within your projected budget (3) you will have to invest some of your own money into the business (4) you must demonstrate that you have good managerial skills or prior business experience (5) and finally you must show that you have a viable plan in which to repay the funds in a timely manner.

If you have a designated start date for your business and you plan on obtaining a loan guaranteed by the SBA, you may need to make some adjustments as the lending process can be somewhat lengthy; anywhere from six to nine months.

Counseling is provided free of charge to those who are starting a business or those who are already in business and experiencing difficulty. The service is provided through the Service Corp. of

Retired Executives (SCORE). These are individuals who are there primarily to work with you and assist you in all phases of your business.

The SBA has a wonderful calendar of excellent pre-business workshops. There you get to meet and interact with other individuals who are experiencing exactly what you are. The SBA generally puts out a calendar listing dates and times of various classes offered. There is often a nominal fee for each class.

When you call or write the SBA, ask them about the other valuable services they offer, such as Small Business Development Center (SBDC), Small Business Institues (SBI).

The SBA is known for their publications. They offer information on all types of topics in business. You may obtain a free copy of their brochure which lists the publications by calling your local SBA office, or call the SBA Answer Desk located in Washington, D.C., at 800-368-5855.

"The Importance of Being Professional"

5 | The Importance of Being Professional

IMAGE

What comes to mind when you think of the following businesses: Apple Computer, Baskin-Robbins Ice Cream, Domino's Pizza, Ford Motor Company, Estee Lauder Cosmetics, Hallmark Cards, Hewlett-Packard, Mrs. Field's Cookies, Reader's Digest, and Walt Disney? Do you think *home-based businesses*? No! Well, you should—all of the above-mentioned companies started right from their homes. Each and every one of these businesses are extremely successful, and each one portrays an image of success. There should be no doubt in your mind that you too can achieve major success as a home-based business.

These businesses have excellent reputations and very positive images, but it didn't happen by accident. Their images were well thought-out and planned.

What do you want people to think of you and your business? Do you want them to think that you are reliable, dependable, knowledgeable and trustworthy? Study other sewing professionals to determine what it is you like or dislike about their businesses, and think of what images come to your mind as you observe them. Think of the image you want to give *your* clients and of the ways you can go about doing so.

If you want a positive image for your business, make sure that every aspect of your business is consistent with what you are trying to portray. This means from the name of your business, your stationery and business cards, to the office and sewing studio, the service you give the client and the quality of work you produce, to how you dress and carry yourself...all of these elements must be in harmony with each other. The whole package has to fit.

In order to achieve a professional image and gain respect, you must be believable to your clients. Attention to the most minor detail is a must.

You must exude confidence in yourself and your business as well. This only comes when you believe in yourself. In the initial stages, careful planning and research will give you a great deal of confidence. Do not sacrifice in either area.

When you have confidence, you come across as professional and capable. Your clients will have confidence in your ability to operate your business, and will view you as being serious. They will also see you as being successful, and everyone wants to be with a winner. No one has to know that you are just getting started. The poise and self-control that you will gain through proper planning and research will make you appear as though you have been in business all your life!

PROPER CLIENT INTERACTION

Women all over the world share a common bond...the love of fashion. Fashion quietly makes a statement about who you are, and your status in life. The first impression you receive regarding an individual comes from their outward appearance.

Billions of dollars are spent each year by consumers to keep abreast of the latest fashion trends, whether it is buying ready-to-wear from major department and specialty stores, or having clothing custom tailored from the leading sewing professionals. Women are fascinated with fashion. These women carry their enthusiasm regarding fashion throughout every aspect of their lives, from their husband and children, to the decor of their homes...every aspect must be fashionable.

These women are sophisticated shoppers, and they value their individuality. For this reason, a number of fashion-forward women choose to lead rather than follow by having their clothing custom made, for both themselves and their families. They think nothing of having the interior of their homes artfully done by one of the sewing professionals specializing in home decor. They are part of an undying breed of women who uphold the saying "Born to Shop."

A number of sewing professionals are enjoying tremendous success as a result of this new attitude on the part of women to take control in decision-making regarding their wardrobes. They will no longer allow department stores to dictate styles, color and fabrics—these women are *in charge.* Speaking about this new breed of women leads us to the point where we will discuss proper client interaction.

In any business, especially a sewing business, when you have the good fortune to be on the receiving end of a profitable trend, it's important that you understand your clients' needs.

Not only do you need to understand their needs, you will also need to inform them about your business and how it functions.

From the time of the initial phone call, it is your job to determine if you can meet the client's needs. When the client calls, you should ask them a series of questions in order to determine their needs. A good tool to use is a Client Call Sheet (see the example on the following page). The client call sheet will help walk you through the telephone interview process.

Note—The Client Call Sheet will:
1. Help you track referrals
2. Determine clients' needs
3. Inform you of clients' knowledge regarding hiring a sewing professional
4. Prevent overlooking pertinent details

CLIENT CALL SHEET

NAME_____DATE_____
ADDRESS_____
HOME PHONE_____WORK_____
REFERRED BY_____

GARMENT/S_____
DATE NEEDED_____APPT TIME_____

QUESTIONS

DO YOU EXPERIENCE DIFFICULTY FINDING CLOTHING THAT WILL FIT?
_____

PREVIOUSLY WORKED WITH DRESSMAKER YES_____ NO_____

WHAT DID YOU LIKE OR DISLIKE ABOUT THE EXPERIENCE? _____
_____

RETAIL SIZE_____PATTERN SIZE_____

PURCHASED FABRIC_____

PATTERN_____

NOTIONS_____

EXPLAIN FEES: CONSULTATION_____ DEPOSITS_____

FABRIC/NOTIONS FEES:_____

MAIL INFO: YES_____ NO_____ SET APPT_____YES_____NO

COMMENTS:

You will want to track where you get the majority of your clients. This information is vitally important if you are spending money on advertisement. The section *Referred By* is used for this purpose.

The next section will answer the question of whether you specialize in the client's needs and if so, whether or not you are able to meet the date needed. If you cannot do so, you don't need to go any further, however, be sure that you get the client's name and address if you keep a mailing list.

The *Questions* section will serve to help you get acquainted with the client and determine if she has ever worked with a sewing professional. Here is where you can take the opportunity to give her a brief overview of your services. You can go into more detail during the face-to-face interview. The following is an example of how you might explain the initial face-to-face interview/consultation process to your prospective client.

"Mrs. Jones, the consultation will take place in two phases. The first is what I refer to as the *Clerical Phase*. This is where we go over the contract and any questions you might have regarding my services."

Assuming you are charging a consultation fee you would say, "During this phase I will credit your account and give you a written receipt for the consultation fee and any deposits for labor, fabric and notions. The second phase, which is referred to as the *Creative Phase*, takes place in my sewing studio. This is where the fun begins. We will go over your choice of fabric and patterns. An extensive line of pattern catalogs are available for your convenience as well as fabric swatches. Once you have selected your pattern and fabric, a complete set of measurements will be taken. Next, the date is set for your first fitting as well as the date to pickup your garment."

This puts the client at ease. They now have a mental picture of what will take place. Clients feel more at ease when they know what to expect. It builds confidence in you, and it proves to the client that you are professional.

The last section is entitled *Explain Fees*. This section is a reminder to explain pertinent details such as fees for consultation, deposits for fabric and notions, and to mail information if needed. Simply stated, this section is a checklist to insure that you have covered all important information. For example, if an appointment is not scheduled at that time, you may elect to send information regarding your business. This section can serve as a reminder to do so.

Lastly, if all systems are go, the form asks if you will set an appointment. If so, check the appropriate space, go back to the second section and index the appointment time.

You can gain a lot of information about a client during the initial telephone interview. Any information that will assist you in meeting the client's needs should be jotted down under the section for *Comments*.

After completing the telephone interview and indexing the appointment date into your daily planner and three-month calendar, file the form away in a folder titled "Client Call Sheets."

To help you save time and be prepared for

interviews, you should prepare folders ahead of time with all needed forms. Listed below are forms that are used and kept in packets for new clients (to order any of these forms, refer to the ordering information at the end of this book).

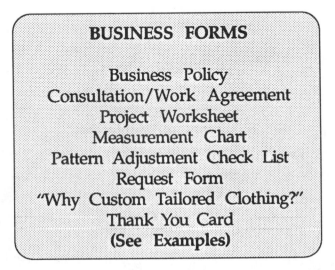

BUSINESS FORMS

Business Policy
Consultation/Work Agreement
Project Worksheet
Measurement Chart
Pattern Adjustment Check List
Request Form
"Why Custom Tailored Clothing?"
Thank You Card
(See Examples)

Let's assume that you have completed a telephone interview in which you have established that you can meet the client's needs, and you have set the appointment. You should be prepared to greet the client, and you should have a new client folder ready to go, complete with the proper forms. Now the moment of truth—your client will be arriving for her first consultation with you.

THE INTERVIEW
You are seated across the desk from your client, you have greeted her and made her comfortable. At this point you should give the client your Business

Policy, have her look it over, and ask if there are any questions (see example on Page 28). If so, address any concerns that she may have. It is very important that you spend time making sure the client fully understands how you operate. You can prevent future problems if you invest that little ounce of time during this phase, and your client will appreciate your concern for her well-being.

Next, you should give her the Consultation/Work Agreement and Measurement Chart. Have her fill out the top section of each, and sign and date the bottom of the Consultation/Work Agreement (see example on page 125). Ask her if she understands the Business Policy, then have her initial the section on the Consultation/Work Agreement where it says "Business Policy Received." Once this is completed, it is time to give her a receipt for the consultation fee (see page 126 for examples of receipts). It should be noted that if your client has decided on a particular fabric and pattern, you can determine the complete charges at this time. You may collect the deposits for labor and any notions you will furnish and include them on the receipt. Don't forget to give her credit on the Consultation/Work Agreement form as well.

Some sewing professionals have great difficulty asking for money. Remember—you are providing a service, and your time has a premium on it. If you have communicated properly with your client, she will expect to pay these fees. The easiest way to handle this procedure is to say to the client as you reach for your receipt book, "Will you be paying by cash, or would you prefer to write a check?" Keep a pleasant expression on your face, you aren't doing the client an injustice, you are simply preforming a natural procedure in the course of conducting business. Remember to exude confidence. Give yourself permission to be paid for services rendered. You are worth it. Keep in mind that the client must feel that you are, or she wouldn't have booked the appointment.

Once you have completed what is referred to as the Clerical Phase, you can then work with the client on the part that you both will enjoy...the Creative Phase. This will give you a chance to get acquainted with the likes and dislikes of your client.

Ask the client her preference in patterns. After she's indicated her preference, give her the pattern book of her choice and a *Request Form* so that she may jot down her choices of patterns complete with the page numbers for review. I find that clients really appreciate little conveniences such as the Request Form; it allows them to browse through the pattern book and not lose their reference points. This helps the client in the process of selection, and often results in multiple projects for you. An example of the Request Form appears on the next page:

REQUEST FORM

Please use this form to jot down the patterns you find appealing. This form will serve to help you review those styles you have selected. To list patterns and styles follow the example given below.

EXAMPLE:	PATTERN	STYLE NUMBER	PAGE
	Simplicity	8347	168
	McCalls	3506	610
	Butterick	5702	305
	Vogue	7641	222

PATTERNS	STYLE NUMBER	PAGE

Once the client has made her choices, the next step is to assist her in selecting the proper fabric. Don't forget to go over the notions needed with your client. Make sure she is clear on who will provide what.

We will discuss pricing in greater detail, however, it would suffice to say that you should have your Price Sheet with you during client interviews. If you interact with clients in your office and in your sewing studio, you should have copies of your Price Sheet in both. A client gets the impression that you are professional when you quote prices from specific guidelines rather than off the top of your head.

At this point, you will compute the cost of labor on the patterns chosen for the project. To insure that you do not forget an item, it is best to use a Project Worksheet. On the following page is an example of this form:

Note—The Project Worksheet:
1. Insures that you don't forget to charge for labor-intensive projects
2. Establishes an accurate price for each item of a project
3. Is an excellent tool for calculating alterations

PROJECT WORKSHEET

CLIENT_____   DATE_____
PROJECT_____   PROJECT_____
PATTERN_____VIEW_____   PATTERN_____VIEW_____

SECTION "A"	SECTION "B"
☐ UNLINED_____	☐ UNLINED_____
☐ LINED_____	☐ LINED_____
☐ EXTRA SEAMS_____	☐ EXTRA SEAMS_____
☐ EXTRA DARTS_____	☐ EXTRA DARTS_____
☐ VENTS_____	☐ VENTS_____
☐ PLEATS/TUCKS_____	☐ PLEATS/TUCKS_____
☐ GATHERS_____	☐ GATHERS_____
☐ ZIPPER_____	☐ ZIPPER_____
☐ POCKETS_____	☐ POCKETS_____
☐ WELT_____	☐ WELT_____
☐ FLAP_____	☐ FLAP_____
☐ BUTTONHOLES_____	☐ BUTTONHOLES_____
☐ BOUND_____	☐ BOUND_____
☐ BUTTONS_____	☐ BUTTONS_____
☐ COVERED_____	☐ COVERED_____
☐ BELT_____	☐ BELT_____
☐ BELT LOOPS_____	☐ BELT LOOPS_____
☐ COVERED BUCKLE_____	☐ COVERED BUCKLE_____
☐ TOPSTITCHING_____	☐ TOPSTITCHING_____
☐ SHOULDER PADS_____	☐ SHOULDER PADS_____
☐ CLOSURES_____	☐ CLOSURES_____
☐ PLAIDS_____	☐ PLAIDS_____
☐ STRIPES_____	☐ STRIPES_____
☐ LACE_____	☐ LACE_____
☐ PIPING_____	☐ PIPING_____
☐ BEADING_____	☐ BEADING_____
☐ QUILTING_____	☐ QUILTING_____
☐ COLOR BLOCKING_____	☐ COLOR BLOCKING_____
☐ WEARABLE ART_____	☐ WEARABLE ART_____
☐ PATTERN DESIGN_____	☐ PATTERN DESIGN_____
☐ PATTERN COPY_____	☐ PATTERN COPY_____
☐ OTHER_____	☐ OTHER_____
☐ _____	☐ _____
☐ _____	☐ _____

LABOR TOTALS

Section "A" $_____
Section "B" $_____
GRAND TOTAL $_____

NOTE: Use a separate section for each item. For a suit use Section "A" for the Jacket and Section "B" for the skirt.

The Project Worksheet is easy to use. You will obtain the figures from the Price Sheet. You should begin by filling out the top section, client's name and date, type of project (dress, pants, etc.), pattern and view. Put the base price of the garment on the appropriate line. It will be either unlined or lined. This price will also come from your price sheet. Review the pattern for any extra labor-intensive details such as pleats, gathers, bound buttons, welt pockets, etc.; and put these figures on the appropriate lines and compute the total. Take the labor totals from the Project Worksheet and transfer them to your Consultation/Work Agreement. Before giving the client the total, be sure to double check the figures for notions, fabric and labor. It is imperative that all figures be accurate, as this form will serve as the primary source for the preparation of the invoice. If you do not have all the figures, give the client the figures you have and an estimate of the remainder. Make a note to follow-up with exact prices on the remaining figures for the purchase of such items as fabric and notions. Explain the importance of pre-shrinking, and document the client's preference. Depending upon your field of specialty, you may need to explain other items of importance relating to the project.

If the client has purchased fabric in advance, check the fabric for flaws, and be sure to measure and record the yardage in the presence of the client. It is a good idea to label any fabric, patterns and notions given to you by your clients.

The client's measurements should be taken at this time. Some clients tend to be quite modest. If you aren't sure, offer to excuse yourself while the client disrobes for measurements. Use a measurement chart that you feel comfortable with. I have discovered that sewing professionals have very interesting ways of recording clients' measurements. I consulted with one sewing professional who writes the measurements on a sheet of paper without the benefit of a guide. She claims that she has been doing this for twenty years, and hasn't missed a beat yet!

I have come to appreciate the fact that you should leave nothing to chance. It's easy to overlook a certain measurement if you do not follow a system. You are busy working with the client and trying to establish some degree of comfort as you are taking the necessary measurements, and it is not unlikely that you will forget a vital measurement if you aren't following a guide.

You never want to inconvenience a client by having them return for measurements that should have been completed accurately in the beginning. Clients are hiring you to do a professional job, and that means paying attention to details. To assist you in this process, see the following Measurement Chart sample on the next page.

Note—The Measurement Chart:
1. Serves as a guide during the measurement process
2. Will prevent you from overlooking a specific measurement

Measurement Chart

NAME_____ DATE_____
ADDRESS_____ PHONE_____
CITY_____ STATE_____ ZIP_____

TYPE	RIGHT	LEFT	PATTERN	ADJUST +/-
NECK WIDTH				
HIGH BUST				
FULL BUST				
BUST POINT TO BUST POINT				
BUST DEPTH				
FRONT WAIST LENGTH				
SHOULDER LENGTH				
SHOULDER WIDTH (FRONT)				
SHOULDER SLOPE (FRONT)				
WAIST				
CENTER BACK LENGTH				
SHOULDER EXPANSION				
SHOULDER WIDTH (BACK)				
SHOULDER SLOPE (BACK)				
UPPER ARM				
ELBOW				
SHOULDER TO ELBOW				
SHOULDER TO WRIST				
WRIST				
HIGH HIP				
HIP				
HIP DEPTH				
CROTCH				
THIGH				
PANT LENGTH				
SKIRT LENGTH				
DRESS LENGTH				

Once you have successfully completed all the measurements and gone over the Consultation/ Work Agreement, ask the client once again if there are any questions. If there are none, then set the date for her fitting and subsequent pickup date. Sign and date the form and give the client a copy; file the original in the client's folder.

Make sure that you record the dates for fitting and pickup in your daily planner. It is a good idea to keep at least a three month, master project calendar. This will allow you to determine work in progress at a glance, thus avoiding overbooking. See Chapter Six for more on the Three-Month Calendar.

There are some sections of the Consultation/ Work Agreement that are particularly helpful. First, there is the section that asks about birthdays and anniversaries. This section is used to surprise clients during these special times. The dates can be stored in your computer and checked at the end of each month. Cards sent acknowledging special events such as birthdays and anniversaries are a nice touch. I really appreciate my clients, and I enjoy sending them cards.

The second section is regarding consultation fees. The first hour's consultation fee is waived and applied toward the client's bill when they book a project. However, the subsequent hour(s) consultation fees are not waived and will be charged directly to the client's bill as discussed and stated in the Business Policy. The reason this form is entitled Consultation/Work Agreement is because on occasion, a client will only want to consult with you, and this avoids having too many forms.

There are three forms left in the Client Folder

that have not yet been discussed, and they are the Pattern Adjustment Check List, the "Why Custom Tailored Clothing?" sheet and a Thank You Card.

For the most part, the Pattern Adjustment Check List is used during the pattern preparation phase prior to layout. This form acts as an insurance policy against overlooking any needed adjustments. It is placed in the client's folder initially so that it is on hand, and it saves time when working on the client's project. This form is especially useful if you hire employees or subcontractors. You will need to be aware of the changes made on clients' projects. Remember—you are responsible for the final outcome of the client's project regardless of who actually performs the work...it's *your* business! See the following page for an example of the Pattern Adjustment Check List:

Note—The Pattern Adjustment Check List will:

1. Serve as a system of checks and balances for pattern preparation
2. Prevent you from overlooking needed pattern adjustments
3. Serve as an ideal form for those who hire employees or subcontractors

---

PATTERN ADJUSTMENT CHECK LIST

CLIENT_____ PATTERN_____
DATE_____ PROJECT_____
COMPLETED BY_____

LIST CHANGES MADE

NECK_____

BACK WAIST LENGTH_____

BUST
_____

SHOULDER WIDTH_____

SHOULDER SLOPE_____

UPPER ARM WIDTH_____

ARM
LENGTH_____

WAIST _____

HIP
_____

CROTCH_____

THIGH _____

OTHER _____

_____

HEM LENGTH

PANT _____

SKIRT _____

DRESS _____

_____

COMMENTS/NOTES

The "Why Custom Tailored Clothing?" sheet is a subliminal advertisement piece which is used in a variety of ways. Occasionally it is used as a direct mail piece. It is always given to the client during the Clerical Phase of the initial interview along with the

Business Policy. Remember—you must inform your clients, and this piece validates why your services are valuable.

At first glance, you might think this piece is too wordy and clients won't read it. You will be surprised. Follow the form as the bold captions are explained, and you will began to see the logic:

WHY CUSTOM TAILORED CLOTHING?

Create a wonderful wardrobe by having your clothing custom tailored. Don't let the department stores dictate your since of style. By having clothing custom tailored, you select the style, color, and fabrication...and get the proper **FIT!**

So often, we feel obligated to purchase clothing that simply does not fit. It is either too large or too small, too short or too long! Thus, creating a purchase that gets worn once, maybe twice, and ultimately lost in our closet forever. **"NO-FIT-NO-WEAR"**. Sure, we wear it once out of guilt, after that we feel justified in forgetting we ever purchased it!

There are a number of benefits derived from having your clothing custom tailored. Clothing is personalized for your particular body type....your personal style....color and fabrication. It allows you to be in total control.

My clients have become so particular that they simply refuse to allow department stores to have control over wardrobe decisions. **THEY CHOOSE TO HAVE THEIR CLOTHING CUSTOM TAILORED.**

If you have a strong desire to control your fashion statement, but feel insecure due to lack of knowledge regarding proper style for your particular body type, or the appropriate color or fabrication, **I CAN HELP!** I meet with my clients in the privacy of my office and sewing studio, where all decisions are made in a comfortable,and relaxing environment. Through my knowledge and expertise, I can assist you in making those delicate decisions. Wardrobe consultation can be extremely beneficial and fun. Before **"YOU"** know it, you will be an expert!

I carry a wide selection of pattern catalogs, such as McCall's, Simplicity, New Look, Style, Vogue, Butterick and Burda, or we can custom design an outfit to your specification.

I WELCOME THE OPPORTUNITY TO TALK WITH YOU. For your convenience I have available "My Business Policy." For further information or to schedule an appointment, you may contact me, **BARBARA WRIGHT SYKES,** at 714-464-0078.

At the top of the form it asks the question "Why Custom Tailored Clothing?" The next bold caption says "Fit" which answers the question. The following caption drives the point home: "No-Fit-No-Wear." The next phrase was designed to arouse the curiosity regarding who: "They Choose To Have Their Clothing Custom Tailored." From there, it flows in a series of direct statements... "I Can Help!", "You", "I Welcome The Opportunity To Talk With You", and finally, it brings them to the contact line: "Barbara Wright Sykes, 714-464-0078."

With this type of advertisement, there is a lot being said. To insure that you do not have to discount your message, you must choose a way to capture the client's attention and inform them while doing so. If you can arouse their curiosity, chances are they will read the entire article; and the good news is even if they do not read the entire article they will still get the message through the bold captions if you design it properly. We are constantly influenced through subliminal advertisement. There is no reason why it can't work for your business.

The last form is the Thank You Card. A computer was used to generate this sample Thank You Card. This allows the opportunity of personalizing each and every card. I don't feel that putting "Thank You" at the bottom of my invoice is sufficient. Within the same week the client picks up their project, a Thank You Card is addressed and dropped into the mail. It is a nice personal touch, and clients

of mine have called to say how much they appreci-
ated receiving the card.

I am more concerned about my clients than just
what they can do for my business. I enjoy making
them happy. I go the extra distance; and I feel good
for having done so. Here is a sample of one of my
Thank You Cards:

The Fitting Appointment

When a client comes for the fitting appointment, make sure that your sewing studio is in order.
The day prior to the appointment, have the client's
folder on hand and: (1) Check any notations you
have made on the pattern adjustment sheet, (2)
Compare them to her measurement chart, and (3)
Inspect the garment to insure that you have covered every detail. There could be pertinent notes

jotted down regarding the fitting appointment, and you don't want to miss a *single* detail.

During the fitting process, you should pay careful attention to the client's needs. Often, clients will have preconceived ideas as to what they should look like, so try to be patient as you work through the fitting process.

If a client suggests that you change design details that have not been accounted for in the contract, you must gently remind them of the agreement, and suggest that you would be delighted to make the necessary design changes, however you will have to charge them for doing so.

If the client's request is just a matter of fit, then it is the responsibility of the sewing professional to make the necessary corrections. Jot down every pertinent detail relevant to meeting the client's needs.

After making sure the client is satisfied with what will be done, review the pickup date with her. When clients are pleased with your services, they are eager to continue doing business with you; so take advantage of every opportunity to make your client a satisfied customer. When you are confirming the pickup appointment, ask if you should allow extra time during the pickup appointment to schedule future projects.

If you have worked with a client for some time and have a good grasp of her likes and dislikes, it would be wise to have patterns and fabric swatches available to inspire her to book another consultation. Everyone enjoys being looked after, and having your own personal wardrobe consultant is quite chic.

Pickup Appointment

Always give yourself enough time to review the client's entire file for purchases you have made on her behalf; as well as deposits, fabric, and notions received from the client, and any additional fees such as pre-shrinking charges. Make sure *everything* has been accounted for.

Next, refer to the Consultation\Work Agreement once again to prepare the invoice, and compare it against the Project Worksheet for accuracy. This would be a good time to address the envelope for the Thank You Card and sign it. If you operate your business by computer, make the necessary entries to reflect completion of the contract. Although the invoice is prepared from the information on the Consultation/Work Agreement, you should file a copy in the client's folder for future reference. Please see the following page for a sample invoice.

Note—Before preparing the invoice, be sure to:
1. Review the figures on the Project Worksheet
2. Review the figures on the Consultation/ Work Agreement against the Project Work sheet, and all receipts for the client's project

---

INVOICE

NAME:
DATE:

DESCRIPTION	CHARGES	CREDITS	BALANCE
CONSULTATION			
LABOR			
FABRIC\NOTIONS			
SUB-TOTALS			
TAX			
TOTALS			
BALANCE DUE			$_____

THANK YOU

When the client arrives to pickup the garment, make sure she is completely satisfied before you present the invoice. If the client is pleased with the project and has no objections, you may introduce the invoice for final payment. At this point, you should feel very confident in asking the client for

the final payment on her project. You have successfully performed a service and your client is happy,
now you will be rewarded for having done so.
Remember to exude confidence and keep a pleasant expression as you reach for your receipt book!
By now you should be comfortable saying, "Will
that be cash, or would you prefer to write a check?"

PRICING: DON'T FLY BY THE SEAT OF YOUR PANTS!

Pricing seems to be a stressful issue for most
entrepreneurs. It's almost as if they are embar-
rassed to ask for what they are worth. Some have
difficulty assigning value to their services. Perhaps
it is because they perform a service that makes it
difficult to determine a price. For the most part, it is
a matter of having the right frame of mind and a
thorough understanding of pricing. As was mentioned earlier, you must give yourself permission to
be paid what you are worth.

In this chapter, we will see the relationship
between the Project Worksheet and the Price Sheet
for establishing a final price for labor. Before beginning, let's examine how a Price List is developed.

Chapter One provided a method to assess which
tasks you liked and which ones you disliked, thus
providing a foundation for identifying the appropriate category best suited for you.

Now that you have selected the field most
favorable to you, it is time to list the various projects
related to that field and assign a value to each.

Pricing Methods

Some sewing professionals use the *flat fee method*, others elect to charge *by the hour*, and some use the *integrated pricing system*. A flat fee pricing policy gives a specific price for each item, for example a pillow would be $20 dollars, a bedspread $200 dollars, and so on. The only problem with the flat fee method is that often sewing professionals don't allow for projects that are more detailed, and they end up underpricing the project. The flat fee method may not leave flexibility for labor-intensive tasks.

The hourly rate method establishes a set fee to be charged per hour for completion of projects. Some sewing professionals object to the hourly method because they don't want clients to know their hourly fees.

The integrated pricing system assigns base value for a project, and it also allows you to add charges to the basic price for specific design details and labor-intensive tasks. Take for instance, a client brings you a project that has a lot of pleats. This takes more time, and you can account for it by adding the additional labor to the base price.

The integrated pricing system also gives the client some flexibility over pricing. If a client wants a suit made and it seems too costly with welt pockets at $10 dollars each (see the Sample Price List for welt pockets), they can simply elect to eliminate the welt pockets and still have their suit made well within their budget. This method also allows the sewing professional room to charge for projects that are more detailed and labor-intensive, and it maintains discretion regarding your hourly rate; not to mention the satisfaction it gives clients to have some control over pricing.

The Sample Price List

The Sample Price List was made based upon a *time/motion study* (to be discussed in detail in Chapter 6) conducted for a sewing professional who desired to earn $19.00 dollars per hour and use the integrated pricing method. Based on what the market would bear at that time, there were some modifications made to reflect market trends. Following is the three-page, Sample Price List.

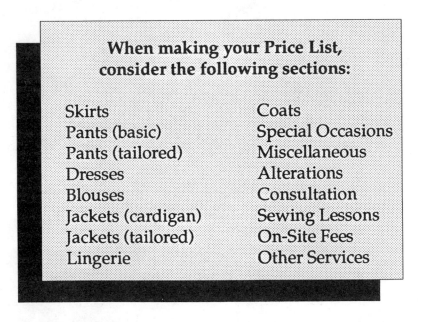

When making your Price List, consider the following sections:

Skirts	Coats
Pants (basic)	Special Occasions
Pants (tailored)	Miscellaneous
Dresses	Alterations
Blouses	Consultation
Jackets (cardigan)	Sewing Lessons
Jackets (tailored)	On-Site Fees
Lingerie	Other Services

SAMPLE PRICE LIST

	UNLINED	LINED
SKIRTS		
BASIC W/O BAND (ELASTIC)	40.00	50.00
(W/INSIDE POCKETS)	47.00	57.00
(ELASTIC W/INSIDE PCKTS/BAND)	52.00	62.00
BASIC STRAIGHT	50.00	60.00
(W/INSIDE POCKETS)	57.00	67.00
WELT POCKETS (EACH)	10.00	10.00
PLEATED	57.00	67.00
ADDED FEATURES: PRICE SUBJECT TO DESIGN DETAILS		
PANTS		
BASIC W/O BAND (ELASTIC)	40.00	50.00
(W/INSIDE POCKETS)	47.00	57.00
(ELASTIC W/INSIDE PCKTS/BAND)	52.00	62.00
WELT POCKETS (EACH)	10.00	10.00
TAILORED W/O PCKTS	50.00	60.00
(WITH INSIDE POCKETS)	57.00	67.00
WELT POCKETS (EACH)	10.00	10.00
FRONT FLY ZIPPER	8.00	8.00
ADDED FEATURES: PRICE SUBJECT TO DESIGN DETAILS		
DRESSES		
BASE PRICE	60.00	70.00

ADDED FEATURES (POCKETS, LACE OVERLAY, COLOR BLOCKING, WEARABLE
ART, BUTTONHOLES, QUILTING, BEADING, ETC.)
PRICE SUBJECT TO DESIGN DETAILS
COMBINING PATTERNS, $19.00 PER HOUR

	UNLINED	LINED
BLOUSES		
BASIC (STARTS AT)	40.00	50.00
SHORT SLEEVE W/OPENING	45.00	55.00
LONG SLEEVE (BASIC)	50.00	60.00
TAILORED	57.00	67.00
ADDED FEATURES: PRICE SUBJECT TO DESIGN DETAILS		
JACKETS		
CARDIGAN (BASIC)	70.00	80.00
W/INSIDE POCKETS	77.00	87.00
W/PATCH POCKETS	84.00	94.00
WELT POCKETS (EACH)	10.00	10.00
VENT, FLAP (EACH)	7.00	7.00
ADDED FEATURES: PRICE SUBJECT TO DESIGN DETAILS		

1

SAMPLE PRICE LIST

JACKETS	UNLINED	LINED
TAILORED (BASIC)	90.00	100.00
W/PATCH POCKETS	97.00	107.00
VENT, FLAP (EACH)	7.00	7.00
WELT POCKETS (EACH)	10.00	10.00

ADDED FEATURES: PRICES SUBJECT TO DESIGN DETAILS

LINGERIE	BASIC	LONG
CAMISOLE:	30.00	
ROBES	40.00	55.00
SLIPS-FULL:	30.00	37.00
SLIPS-HALF:	20.00	27.00

ADDED FEATURES: LACE, APPLIQUES, BEADS, LINING, PIPING, PRICE SUBJECT TO DESIGN DETAIL

COATS		
CARDIGAN	85.00	95.00
SHAWL COLLAR	110.00	120.00
PLEATED COLLAR	120.00	130.00
TAILORED (BASIC)	125.00	135.00
POCKET, VENT, FLAP (EACH)	10.00	10.00
WELT POCKET	10.00	10.00

OTHER ADDED FEATURES: PRICES SUBJECT TO DESIGN DETAILS

SPECIAL OCCASION

PROM	EVENING DRESSES	MOTHER-OF-THE-BRIDE
BRIDES MAIDS	WEDDING GOWNS	COCKTAIL PANT SUITS

PRICES SUBJECT TO DESIGN DETAILS AND FABRICATION SELECTED

MISCELLANEOUS

SHOULDER PADS/UNCOVERED	10.00
SHOULDER PADS/COVERED	15.00
MATCHING PLAIDS	15.00
STRIPES	10.00
SEAMS (ADDITIONAL)	9.00
BOUND BUTTONHOLES (EACH)	10.00
DESIGN CHANGES PER HOUR	19.00
DESIGN LININGS (COATS, JACKETS)	10.00
DESIGN LININGS (DRESSES)	10.00
DESIGN LININGS (SKIRTS, PANTS)	8.00
SIZES OVER EIGHTEEN (18)	15.00
PRE-SHRINKING FABRIC (PER YARD)	1.10
BUTTONHOLES (EACH)	1.50
BUTTONS (EACH)	1.20
COVERED BUTTONS (EACH)	5.00
SNAPS, HOOK/EYE (SET)	2.25
TOPSTITCHING	8.00
BELT/BUCKLE (EACH)	10.00

2

SAMPLE PRICE LIST

ALTERATIONS	UNLINED	LINED
HEMS	12.00	22.00
SLEEVES-HEM	10.00	20.00
SLEEVES REWORK	15.00	25.00
SLEEVES TAPER	10.00	20.00
SHOULDER SEAMS	10.00	20.00
SHOULDER SEAMS W/FACING	15.00	25.00
CROTCH W/O ZIPPER	10.00	20.00
CROTCH W/ZIPPER	20.00	30.00
ZIPPERS (SKIRT/PANTS)	10.00	15.00
ZIPPERS (LEATHER/SUEDE)	13.00	18.00
ZIPPERS (DRESS)	15.00	20.00
SIDE SEAMS W/O BAND (SKIRT)	15.00	25.00
SIDE SEAMS W/O BAND (PANTS)	15.00	25.00
SIDE SEAMS W/BAND (SKIRTS)	20.00	30.00
SIDE SEAMS W/BAND (PANTS)	20.00	30.00

CONSULTATION	PRICES
PER HOUR	19.00
INITIAL (UP-TO-AN-HOUR)	19.00

(WAIVED IF SERVICES ACCEPTED-
AND APPLIED TO FINAL BILL)
NOTE: SEE ON SITE FEES

SEWING LESSONS

PRIVATE (PER HOUR)	19.00	
GROUP RATE 2 TO 10 PEOPLE	15.00	PER PERSON
GROUP RATE 11+ PEOPLE	12.00	PER PERSON

(GROUP SESSIONS ARE HELD ON GROUP SITE)
NOTE: SEE ON SITE FEES

ON SITE FEES

UP TO ONE (1) MILE	2.00
TWO (2) TO FIVE (5) MILES	4.00
SIX (6) TO TEN (10) MILES	6.00
ELEVEN (11) OR MORE (PER MILE)	1.00

How do you use a price list for integrated pricing? Suppose you had a client who wanted a pair of unlined tailored pants, with a front-fly zipper and side pockets. You would: (1) Record the base labor price of $57 for unlined tailored pants with inside pockets on your Project Worksheet, (2) Find the cost of a front-fly zipper (which is $8) and record that on your Project Worksheet as well. The combined fees would give you a total **labor** charge of $65. You would transfer this charge to your Consultation/ Work Agreement under the section for *labor charge*. The rest of the charges for fabric and notions and so on, would be charged directly to the client and would be included in the total price.

Regardless of which method you select, several factors need to be considered. According to the SBA (Small Business Administration) you must factor in several elements, and they are: the costs associated with operating your business (known as *overhead expenses)*, cost of goods sold (or *direct costs*), and your *salary*.

Operating or overhead costs are items such as rent, utilities, advertising, taxes, travel, office/sewing supplies and equipment, upkeep, maintenance, license and permits, etc. Cost of goods sold or direct costs are those items utilized in the production of each project and are billed directly to the client's invoice. Salary is what you are paid for services rendered.

Direct costs are relatively easy to determine. When you purchase items for resale in your business, you log them into your inventory; and you can obtain the cost from your purchase order. For example, in completing a project where you will invoice the client for a zipper, you can get the exact cost from your inventory list or purchase order.

However, overhead expenses are a little more involved. In the beginning it may be somewhat difficult to accurately assess these expenses. You may get some assistance from contacting certain trade associations or network organizations. Often they can give you an idea of what these costs will run. Or, you may average out the expenses that you know and estimate the rest with some research.

You want your business to be profitable, therefore you must account for these expenses. Because there are inherent costs of doing business, the amount you receive for each project is not going to reflect pure profit. The figure will represent the *gross sales*. Consequently, you must deduct overhead and direct expenses to arrive at *net profit* or *net sales*.

In pricing, you must also understand what the market will bear. There is a point at which clients will object to certain price points. It should be pointed out that certain clients will object no matter what the price is. These are individuals who insist on having the last word in all transactions; they simply enjoy negotiating. Recognize these clients for who they are and do not allow their objections to influence your judgement regarding your pricing structure.

Experience has proven that if: (1) your business is run professionally (2) you understand your market, (3) your business image is consistent, and (4) you gain the respect of your clients through proper client interaction, there is generally very little price resistance.

A thorough understanding of your market will be gained through doing your homework. You must understand your potential clients and your competitors. You should examine your competitors' pricing structure; and in doing so, consider whether the business reflects professionalism. Try to assess the type of clientele that particular business maintains. In comparing it to yours, is it consistent in all areas?

A number of sewing professionals tend to feel guilty regarding pricing. This results in underpricing their services. Keep in mind that you are providing the client with a service that is unique, and if you have conveyed your services effectively during the initial contact, the client fully understands how valuable your services are. There is no need to discount your services...under any circumstances.

Pricing Formula

Now that we have all of that in mind how do you arrive at a price? You need to know how long it will take you to perform a task or complete a project. These figures can be determine by conducting a Time and Motion Study. A complete discussion of a Time/Motion Study will be covered in Chapter 6.

You should have a clear understanding of how much it will cost to operate your business, this includes both your direct costs and your overhead costs. Lastly, you must have the total number of hours you will commit to the business. There are four components needed to structure your price list for the integrated pricing system:

1. Total cost of overhead expenses
2. Total hours committed to work
3. Desired salary
4. Hours needed to complete a task

Note: You will invoice direct expenses to the client from your purchase list or inventory sheet.

Let's say that you have decided to use the integrated pricing system, and after doing your homework, you establish that your total overhead cost for a month will be approximately $500, and you wish to have a monthly salary of $2,500. You have committed to work 160 hours a month (using 4 weeks per month at 40 hours per week). Now, let's determine what your hourly rate would have to be to accomplish your goal. Following is a formula to compute the hourly base rate.

OVERHEAD EXPENSES + SALARY
DIVIDED BY HOURS WORKED PER MONTH
=YOUR HOURLY BASE RATE.

In the above example, you would take your overhead expense of $500 and add it to the desired salary of $2,500. The combined figures equal $3,000. You divide your 160 monthly hours committed to work into the $3,000, which would give you your hourly base rate of $18.75. Remember—this does not include direct expenses, which will be billed on a per project basis to the client.
HOURLY BASE RATE

1) $2,500
   + 500
   $3,000

2) **$3,000 Divided by 160 hrs.= $18.75**

In the instance where the client provides all needed fabric and notions, there will be no direct expenses. To keep things simplistic the $18.75 should be rounded off to $19.00 dollars per hour. This becomes the base figure for creating a price list.

Let's say that you have your Time and Motion Chart before you, and you are ready to compute the figures to make up your price list. (See the example of a Time and Motion Chart in Chapter 6)

From your Time and Motion Study, you have discovered that it will take you 7 hours to complete an unlined jacket. To get your total labor cost or base price, you would multiply your hourly rate of $19.00 by the number of hours needed (7) to complete the unlined jacket to get a value of $133.00 dollars for your base price. You apply this same process through the remainder of the items to establish your base price for each item. When you have all of the base prices completed, you can develop your own price sheet. You will need to print at least two copies, one for your sewing studio and the other for your office.

Note: Direct costs will vary from project to project, and you will bill the client for these costs when you utilize the integrated pricing system. If you have direct costs that stay relatively constant, you should make a chart with those items; it will save you the time of looking them up.

For example, if you purchase zippers in bulk from a wholesaler, and you know that the price per zipper is constant, you can create a chart for these types of items. If there are items that will be resold by the yard, such as interfacing, put the price per yard as your constant, so that you only have to multiply the price per yard times the number of yards needed to arrive at the figure to be invoiced back to the client. This will come in handy when quoting direct prices to clients during the initial consultation phase.

SETTING STANDARDS

Any successful business sets standards for its employees. You should think of your business much the same way as you would if you were employed for someone else. Set standards for your business and stick to them. There are two areas in which you should set specific standards, and they are: (1) Performance, and (2) Technical. Just think of it as getting a head start on writing your personnel manual for your future employees.

Performance

When considering what performance standards you should adopt, think of what you would expect of an employee working for you. Build in beginning and ending times as well as times for breaks and lunch. What holidays will you observe? When will you take your vacation? How will you address friends who wish to socialize? Will you entertain unexpected visitors?

Will you apply the guidelines and principles in your business policy to all clients, or will you select those who are your favorites and extend special treatment?

List the ways in which you will measure your performance regarding the completion of projects. How will you receive encouragement during those times when things get tough? You can believe that there will be those times, so plan to guard against giving into to the desire to abandon ship during the storm.

Since you will have no one looking over your shoulder and checking up on you, how will you discipline yourself? What will keep you focused and on track?

Recognize certain behavioral patterns that you may have exhibited in the past when working for others. Identify those that could be a potential problem for you and build in precautionary measures.

All in all, you want to establish rules, regulations and standards that will insure that your performance is and will always be at its optimum level.

Technical

Technological advances have had a tremendous impact on production. Let's look at two areas of major change that have taken place over the years which have had a major influence in the sewing industry.

Through the development of computer technology, we now have computerized sewing machines that have speeded up production tremendously and allowed sewing professionals to perform various tasks that were once reserved only to manufacturers of ready-to-wear. Another major technological advancement is that of the serger. Today, for home sewing professionals, it is the rule rather than the exception to have a serger.

We now use computers as sewing professionals to keep records in our business. Thus, enabling us to provide better and more efficient service to our clients. To further illustrate how valuable computers have become to the sewing industry, in 1991, a major sewing machine company introduced a sewing machine that interfaces with computers. There is software available, and software being developed for the industry. (For further information on ordering software, see order information at the end of this book)

In order to stay current with the marketplace you will have to invest some time in educating yourself on products that will enhance your business.

By attending seminars, and meetings of various trade organizations you will stay abreast of current trends. Subscribing to publications which address major issues in your industry will further enhance your ability to stay on top of key issues of major importance to your business. You will have to build in time for research and development of new products and techniques that are applicable to your particular business.

Not only do you provide a service, you also produce a product, which means that you will need to be aware of service related trends as well as product innovations, and to do so will require some of your precious time. Examine *your* own technological advancements with the industry at large. If you don't measure up, then it is time to make some changes. Remember your clients are expecting you to provide the best that the market has to offer and they will accept no excuses!

CONSULTATION/WORK AGREEMENT

DATE_____ TIME IN_____OUT_____AM/PM
NAME_____
ADDRESS_____
CITY_____ZIP_____
HOME PHONE_____WORK_____
BIRTHDAY_____ANNIVERSARY_____
REFERRED BY_____
_____OFFICE USE_____
CONSULTATION FEE
PAID_____WAIVED/APPLIED: BUSINESS POLICY RECEIVED_____

DATE DUE_____ FITTING DATE_____

AMT. YARDAGE RECEIVED_____   PROJECT_____
CHECKED FOR FLAWS   □ YES   □ NO   PATTERN_____
PRE-SHRINK   □ YES   □ NO   COMMENTS:
□ DRY CLEAN   □ WASH

NOTIONS RECEIVED   □ YES   □ NO

_____
_____
_____

FABRIC\NOTIONS PURCHASED
_____ $_____
_____ $_____
_____ $_____
_____ $_____
_____ $_____
_____ $_____
_____ $_____
_____ $_____
_____ $_____
TOTAL $_____

BASIC LABOR CHARGE $_____
ADDED DESIGN DETAILS
_____ $_____
_____ $_____
_____ $_____
_____ $_____
_____ $_____
TOTAL $_____   CLIENTS SIGNATURE-DATE
CONSULTATION FEE $_____

_____

    CREDITS

1st HOUR WAIVED   <$_____>
DEPOSITS RECEIVED   <$_____>

EXAMPLES OF RECEIPTS

00668

CUSTOMER'S ORDER NO.		DATE				
NAME						
ADDRESS						
CITY, STATE, ZIP						

SOLD BY	CASH	C.O.D.	CHARGE	ON ACCT.	MDSE RETD	PAID OUT

QUAN.	DESCRIPTION	AMOUNT
1		
2		
3		
4		
5		
6		
7		
8		
9		
10		
11		
12		

RECEIVED BY

KEEP THIS SLIP FOR REFERENCE

4989

DATE_____ 19____ NO.

RECEIVED OF_____

ADDRESS_____

_____ $_____

FOR

HOW PAID	BALANCE DUE	
8K826		BY_____

6 Problems You Will Face As A Sewing Professional

Doubt, Fear and Procrastination

The three most common enemies that will rob you and your business of its success are doubt, fear, and procrastination. Being able to recognize the symptoms will be advantageous. Unless you can overcome these problems, they will cause you to become anxious and extremely frustrated. The results can paralyze your ability to complete tasks or goals that are vital to the success of your business.

How do they manifest themselves? You generally find yourself doubting your ability to successfully complete a task or accomplish a goal. Before you realize it, the fear of failure sets in, followed by a general inclination to put things off or not tackle them at all; known as procrastination.

What are some of the obstacles that might cause this kind of reaction?

* Feeling overwhelmed with the number of tasks involved
* Feeling incapable
* Not being accustomed to working alone
* Not having a plan
* Not having control over interruptions
* Underestimating your budget
* Lack of organization
* Feeling that you aren't smart enough
* Feeling you don't measure up to the competition
* Feeling that you can't handle the pressure
* Lack of self-esteem and self-confidence

There are many reasons why people fall prey to doubt, fear and procrastination. However, the good news is that it can be overcome. You must start by resisting the urge to give in to negative thoughts. Open yourself up to *changing* bad habits. Recognize when you are working and when you are wasting valuable time...and **STOP** wasting productive time.

In the beginning, send out announcements to friends and family to let them know that you are an entrepreneur and have set hours for your business, and would love to hear from them **AFTER** hours!

To prevent feeling overwhelmed, get in the habit of dividing your projects into small sections. If you can see small tasks being accomplished, the final project will seem more realistic and therefore less stressful. This method will put an end to the urge to procrastinate. As far as feeling incapable and not having a plan, these feelings should not occur if you follow the step-by-step procedure for your business plan discussed in Chapter 3.

Getting and staying organized will alleviate most of your fears and doubts regarding your ability to become successful. Reread Chapter 1, "Knowing When You Are Ready." It deals with some of the anxiety involved in starting and maintaining a business. Keep this text handy during the times when you feel that you can't go on...reflect on what it will take to keep you hanging in there. YOU CAN DO IT!

TIME MANAGEMENT

Your time has a premium on it. Because your time is so valuable, you must use it wisely. You *are* your business, and your success is dependent upon wise use of your time.

Being in business requires that you wear many different hats; hats ranging from designer to secretary, teacher to student, ; and many others depending upon the nature of your business. You must decide how to divide your time to receive the maximum return on your investment. In order to accomplish this goal, you need to understand the various phases of your particular business.

We will examine these "hats" commonly worn by sewing professionals:

Clerical, Recordkeeping, Interviews, Sewing and Teaching. Accomplishing each task takes a significant amount of time, and time must be allowed to successfully do so. As you read further, try to determine how much time you must allocate daily to each task in order to keep your business healthy. Time management is one of the most crucial factors in scheduling production.

Most sewing professionals only think of the time needed to produce the actual garment and forget that there are additional business task that must receive their time and attention, thus creating problems with production time.

Failing to acknowledge that business-related tasks need to be accounted for also results in the sewing professional overbooking sewing projects and finding that due to other concerns in the business, they are running out of production time.

Clerical

Clerical duties can involve opening, sorting and filing mail; typing, making phone calls to request quotes on supplies, ordering supplies, inputting new client files into the computer, preparing client folders, taking inventory; and the list goes on.

No matter what the task may be, time must be allocated. Decide on a method that works best for you and implement it into your schedule. Perhaps you will take a few minutes a day to return phone calls and sort through daily mail, while you reserve specific days for inventory of supplies.

Some tasks will demand attention on a daily basis, and some can be shifted to designated days. For example, you may find that because of recordkeeping and the preparation of valuable statements, it is better for you to take inventory at the beginning of the month to reflect the previous month's activity.

Recordkeeping

Keeping good records is a must, not only for tracking the progress of your business, but to make sure you are keeping in line with the requirements of the Internal Revenue Service.

Develop a recordkeeping system that works well for you. There are bookkeeping services that will pick up your records and compile them into statements for a nominal fee. You might feel more comfortable giving the entire task to an accountant if you have the funds to do so. Or, you can have your accountant set up your books and instruct you on how to keep records. This will cut down on the fees, and will allow you to enlist their services only for financial statements at certain predetermined intervals.

For most small businesses, there are two important statements that are frequently needed: 1. Profit and Loss, and 2. Balance Sheet.

Some businesses require monthly statements while others have them prepared quarterly or semi-annually.

Another alternative would be to keep receipts in large envelopes by specific accounts. Some examples are: Sales, Expenses, and so on. Or, keep journal entries of business activity to be compiled into reports by your accountant. Lastly, you could purchase a manual accounting system, such as *Ideal's* *"Merchants Bookkeeping & Tax Record"*, at your local stationery store. There are a number of good manual recordkeeping systems available. Check with your local stationery or office supply store.

If you have the use of a computer, a good computer software accounting program works well. However, with the software you should have a working knowledge of accounting. One of the more cost effective systems is *M.Y.O.B.* by Teleware, which is an acronym for *Mind Your Own Business*. This program even allows you to make your own logos for your invoices, letterhead and envelopes. A video tape is also available to help get you started.

At some time during the week, it would be wise to get into the habit of recording the week's activity into a journal or some type of manual bookkeeping system. If you utilize a computer, input all transactions into your accounting software program.

It would be advisable to consult an accountant or tax specialist to assist you in setting up your recordkeeping system, regardless of what type of system you select. Listed on the following page are a few categories or accounts you should keep track of in your recordkeeping system.

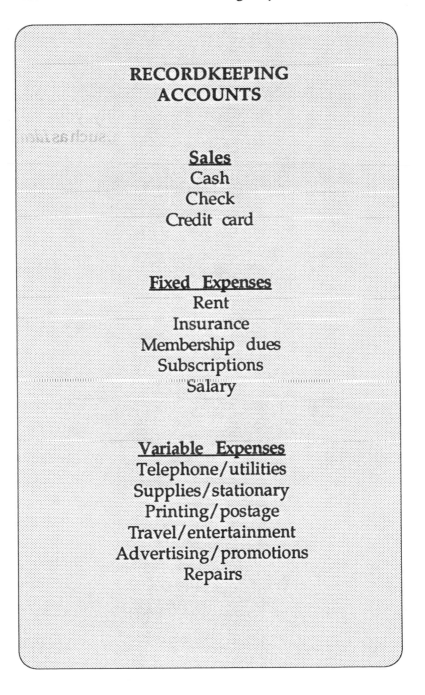

RECORDKEEPING
ACCOUNTS

Sales
Cash
Check
Credit card

Fixed Expenses
Rent
Insurance
Membership dues
Subscriptions
Salary

Variable Expenses
Telephone/utilities
Supplies/stationary
Printing/postage
Travel/entertainment
Advertising/promotions
Repairs

There are certain recordkeeping activities that should take place daily, weekly and monthly. Following are a few pertinent ones:

RECORDKEEPING ACTIVITIES

DAILY

SALES
CASH ON HAND
FILING
PLACING NEW SUPPLIES INTO INVENTORY SYSTEM
LARGE DEPOSITS THAT CAN'T WAIT UNTIL END-OF-THE WEEK
REVIEW AND RECORD ANY MONEY PAID OUT DURING THAT DAY

WEEKLY

ACCOUNTS PAYABLE (PAY THEM IN ORDER TO RECEIVE ANY
   DISCOUNTS)
ACCOUNTS RECEIVABLE (ACCOUNTS WITH PAST DUE BALANCES)
REVIEW PETTY CASH
REVIEW WEEKLY CLIENT CALLS/INTERVIEWS WITH MASTER
   SCHEDULE
RECORD ANY NEW PURCHASES MADE FOR THE BUSINESS
REVIEW PREVIOUS WEEKS SALES VOLUME
PAY SALARY/WAGES (UNLESS PAID BI-MONTHLY OR MONTHLY)
ON THE LAST DAY OF THE WEEK, REVIEW THE NEXT WEEK'S
   SCHEDULE

MONTHLY

RECONCILE BANK ACCOUNT
BALANCE CHECK BOOK
BALANCE LEDGER ACCOUNTS (OR HAVE READY FOR ACCOUNTANT)
PREPARE INCOME AND EXPENSE TOTALS FOR STATEMENTS
REVIEW ACCOUNTS PAYABLE/RECEIVABLE
PREPARE NEEDED PROFIT & LOSS AND BALANCE SHEET STATEMENTS
MAIL TAX PAYMENT TO STATE BOARD OF EQUALIZATION (IF DUE)

Make a list of the various recordkeeping activities that pertain to your specific business and record them under the appropriate categories.

Interviews

In Chapter 5, we discussed the various steps involved in the interview process. The time it will take is controlled largely by you. You don't want to be abrasive to your clients at anytime, but occasionally it will be necessary to gently take control of the conversation when you see it is moving into areas other than business.

You may set an hour per interview if you aren't familiar with how long it will take you to cycle through the two phases of the face-to-face interview. The Clerical Phase and the Creative Phase (see Chapter 5) can be perfected given time and experience. As you become familiar with the majority of your clients you can judge the amount of time needed for the two phases.

You will need to allow more time for first-time clients as there are a number of concerns that need to be addressed. In either case, you must exercise discipline with regard to your time.

Don't forget to figure in time for new telephone contacts, and clients calling with questions regarding their projects. We don't think about it, but these frequent interruptions do take time. It is safer if we factor in a set amount of time just to cover these day-to-day activities.

When you are on production time never answer the phone. All incoming calls can be handled by your answering machine. If you are worried about missing an emergency call, set the volume control where you can hear the messages, and therefore be able to respond to any urgent call.

At the end of the morning's production, approximately fifteen minutes prior to lunch, check all messages and return the important morning calls. Calls from individuals in other time zones should be addressed at this time. If the calls can wait until later in the day, return them when you check your messages at the end of your production day. Allow approximately a half an hour to respond to those important calls depending upon the volume. Over a period of time, you will be able to determine with some degree of accuracy, the time needed for various tasks.

Sewing

Sewing encompasses actual production time. How long will it take you to complete a task in order to finish a project? This information will have been determined from a Time and Motion Study, which we are going to cover in this chapter. This is the basis from which you should schedule or book your projects.

In Chapter 5, we discussed computing the base labor price, by utilizing the time that it takes to complete a certain project. We stated that you must know the hours you will commit to your business for production in order to determine your base price along with other variables. If you will recall, we did not speak of other business-related tasks in the actual time being committed to the business; the time discussed was only in reference to actual production.

As you can see, your time committed to the business will occur in many different areas, and production is just one.

In our earlier example, we stated that we would commit to 40 hours a week for production. Taken into consideration that there are other tasks performed in the operation of a business, we would need to add additional hours to cover these tasks. Let's say that we will allocate 20 hours to other business-related tasks; add that to the 40 hours production time and we have a total time committed to the business of 60 hours per week.

Our new figure translates to a 12-hour work day. This figure holds true for many entrepreneurs. It is rare that a self-employed individual finds herself working the standard 40 hour work-week.

The above scenario serves as a reminder to allow sufficient time for production of sewing of projects and to be very careful not to leave out the time needed for other business-related tasks. Keep your production or sewing time purely for that purpose; try not to combine the two.

Teaching

If you offer sewing lessons, whether private or group, the time must be allotted.

Your fees will have to be structured in such a way that the time needed for preparation and teaching will produce the needed results to contribute to the monthly salary you desire.

For example, you have decided that you will allow 8 hours a week for teaching and preparation. You will have to determine what that time translates to in dollars and cents. If you were in production for 8 hours you would earn $19 per hour. For 8 hours of teaching and preparation you must receive at least $19 dollars per hour for it to be worth your while.

On your master planner or monthly schedule, you would put in the hours each week that are to be dedicated to teaching and the preparation that goes along with it. These hours should be subtracted from your available hours for production. Again, make sure that the end justifies the means. It is not difficult to have a healthy balance between the two, however, one must not occur at the expense of the other. Your goal is to make the best use of your time and get the maximum return on your investment while doing so.

Other

There may be other revenue-producing endeavors you can take advantage of, some more lucrative than others. Treat them all the same in terms of their ability to contribute to the overall profitability of your business.

Note: Do not forget your Direct Cost and Overhead. Refer to the section in Chapter 5 on Pricing.

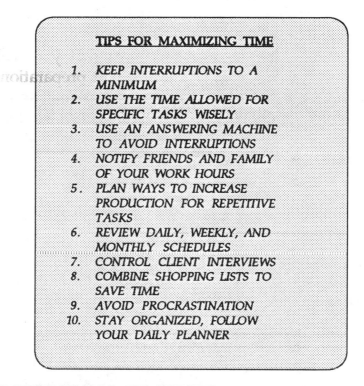

TIPS FOR MAXIMIZING TIME

1. KEEP INTERRUPTIONS TO A MINIMUM
2. USE THE TIME ALLOWED FOR SPECIFIC TASKS WISELY
3. USE AN ANSWERING MACHINE TO AVOID INTERRUPTIONS
4. NOTIFY FRIENDS AND FAMILY OF YOUR WORK HOURS
5. PLAN WAYS TO INCREASE PRODUCTION FOR REPETITIVE TASKS
6. REVIEW DAILY, WEEKLY, AND MONTHLY SCHEDULES
7. CONTROL CLIENT INTERVIEWS
8. COMBINE SHOPPING LISTS TO SAVE TIME
9. AVOID PROCRASTINATION
10. STAY ORGANIZED, FOLLOW YOUR DAILY PLANNER

SCHEDULING PROJECTS

It's not difficult to successfully schedule projects, it just requires you to follow certain guidelines. Don't schedule more projects than you can actually complete—keep in mind how long it will take you to complete each project. Have a clear understanding of just how much time you have committed to production of projects per day, week and month. This is accomplished through the use of a three-month calendar scheduling process, which will be discussed later in this chapter.

HOW MANY CAN I SUCCESSFULLY COMPLETE?

Your ability to produce certain items in a short period of time will depend on your skill level. The more often you perform a task, the better you become. Repetition helps familiarize you with a task and increase your speed. The Time and Motion Study will help you to evaluate and keep an ongoing tally of the time you take to complete tasks and projects.

The Time and Motion Study

Simply stated, a Time and Motion Study is a study to determine how long it will take you to complete certain tasks involved in garment construction in order to earn a profit. You can perform a time and motion study on any task. However, for now it is important to establish production time for sewing purposes.

It is relatively easy to complete a Time and Motion Study. In fact, you can do it without the assistance of anyone other than yourself. The study serves two purposes (1) It will serve as the basis for building an hourly base labor price. and (2) It will tell you how many garments or tasks you can complete in a given time period.

To conduct the study, you will need a legal size notepad and a stop watch or some type of timing device with a second hand. You will record start and stop times for each task that you perform. In order for the study to be accurate, you must record stop times for *every* time you stop or have an interruption in the flow of production. Perform a study for the following:

PROJECT AND TASK LIST

INITIAL PREPARATION	CONSTRUCTION	FINISHING
	[As An Item]	
FABRIC PREPARATION	BODICE	HEMS
PATTERN PREPARATION	SLEEVE	BUTTONS
LAYOUT	COLLAR	BUTTONHOLES
CUTTING	FACINGS	HOOK/EYES
MARKING	LINING	TOPSTITCHING
	SKIRT SEAMS/DARTS	PRESSING
	PANT SEAMS/DARTS	
	WAIST BANDS	
	ZIPPER INSERTION	
	[As A Unit]	
	SKIRT	
	PANTS	
	DRESS	
	JACKET	
	BLOUSE	

TIME AND MOTION CHART

TIME		TIME AND MOTION STUDY	TOTAL TIME
START	**STOP**	**PROJECT/TASK** **TYPE: STRAIGHT SKIRT**	
8:15	9:15	SEAMS/DARTS/ZIPPER/PRESS	1 HOUR
9:30	11:30	SEWED LINING, FUSED INTER- FACING TO WAISTBAND, AP- PLIED LABEL, ATTACHED BAND TO SKIRT AND LINING UNIT, PRESS	2
1:15	2:15	HEM BOTH UNITS BUTTON/BUTTONHOLES,PRESS	1
GRAND TOTAL			**4 HOURS**

When you complete the Time and Motion Study there will be a value assigned to each category, and that value will represent how long it will take you to complete each task or project. Make a list compiling all the totals for each category. See the example below.

PRICE LIST WORKSHEET

PROJECT\TASK	TYPE	TOTAL TIME	TOTAL TIME X BASE RATE $19
SKIRT (LINED)	STRAIGHT	4	$ 76.00
SKIRT	STRAIGHT	3	57.00
PANTS (LINED)	PLEATED	5	95.00
DRESS	A-LINED	6	114.00
BLOUSE	SHELL	3	57.00
JACKET (LINED)	TAILORED	7	133.00
JACKET	TAILORED	6	114.00

The Price List Worksheet will be the basis for developing your final price list. See Chapter 5 for an example of a completed SAMPLE PRICE LIST.

The Three-Month Calendar

Insufficient time to complete projects is one of the major problems that occurs as a result of over-booking, and it can happen very innocently. To avoid having this happen, the use of a three-month calendar is a very effective tool.

By maintaining scheduled projects on a three-month calendar, you can easily see what you have on the books and determine how much time you have available to book future projects.

Some projects take two to four weeks and must be accounted for in your planning. By viewing the current month and two months forward, you can get an accurate picture of what you are dealing with in terms of available time. In order for this method to be successful, you must be diligent in recording all activities requiring your time, including those of a personal nature. These can be obtained from your daily planner.

Keep all calendars of past months; it will help you to determine cyclical periods in your business.

YOUR DAILY PLANNER:
"Don't Leave Home Without It!"

As they say in the American Express commercials, "Don't Leave Home Without It!" Think of your daily planner the same way—you must *never* be without it. You never know when you will need to schedule personal or business endeavors. Always keep your daily planner in reach and up-to-date.

There will be instances when you must schedule time for personal matters; this is valuable time that must be deducted from your available time for production in your business. This time must be accounted for on your schedule so that it will not create future mishaps. So often, we forget to consider these minor occurrences; a daily planner will assist in avoiding these problems.

Just as you would your three-month calendar, you must record blocks of time committed to the business into your daily planner, thus avoiding any scheduling disasters.

PERIODIC REVIEW OF PRODUCTION

Over the course of time, things change; you gain more clients or you increase your production speed. You need to monitor both to determine when to make adjustments in your business to account for these changes.

If you discover that you are swamped with work, it might be time to consider expanding your business. (See Chapter Eight) Here is where reviewing your previous production via the use of the three month calendar becomes helpful.

If you find that as a result of increased productivity you are completing projects with time to spare, perhaps you should consider booking more projects. At any rate, a periodic review of production will uncover helpful information to keep your business running properly. A rule of thumb would be to review your production every six months.

7 Successfully Marketing Your Business

The success or failure of any business is predicated upon a clear understanding of the consumer in the marketplace and where the business stands in relation to its competitors.

You would be surprised at the number of individuals who year after year, consistently go into business without any forethought of how their goods and services will meet the needs and wants of the ultimate consumer. Many entrepreneurs have knowledge of marketing theory and concept, and can recite it word for word. How is it possible that they fail in business? Simple...when asked, they say that it is difficult putting theory into practical application. Certain common sense knowledge is overlooked when developing products or services to appeal to consumer needs and wants.

Consumer behavior should be studied in great detail, matching the various needs of the consumer with the goods or services that your business has to offer in the way of satisfying those needs.

"Successfully Marketing Your Business"

The bottom line is that you must develop your ability to become a good investigator. What does it mean to investigate?

Definition: *To search or inquire into with care and accuracy.*

To garner your share of the marketplace, you must actively investigate the consumer and the competitor.

Identifying Your Market

Who will be your customer? Think of your daily activities and the various individuals you come in contact with...attorneys, bankers, clerks, beauticians, teachers, secretaries, doctors, dentists, associates, parents, friends, salespeople; and the list goes on.

Herein lies a great primary source from which to conduct your own market research. Study each group you come in contact with and determine how your business can satisfy their needs.

Formulate and gain answers to questions regarding your potential clientele that will yield the desired results. Understanding what to look for makes observation of consumer behavior quite amusing, especially when it offers your business a greater share of the marketplace.

As you become armed with the knowledge of consumer behavior, this will allow you to identify your customer. Then you must focus on your competition. Is it necessary to study the competition? **ABSOLUTELY!**

If you want to survive in business, be prepared to devote as much time and effort into understanding your competition. You can bet your clients will study your competitor to see whether or not you are offering them the best in goods and services. Consequently, if you are unaware of what your competition is doing, you can't compete...you are out of the game before you begin.

How will you conduct a study of your competition? Make it a priority on your list of "things to do" to develop your own research system aimed at studying your competition. Remember, as consumer behavior changes, so does the behavior of your competition. For this reason, you must keep a finger on the pulse of the marketplace.

Market analysis can be quite involved and somewhat expensive if you hire a professional. For the purpose of a home-based sewing business, you may not need to get quite so involved. However, if you expand your business into a commercial location where competition is fierce, you will need to employ some if not all of the following techniques or hire a professional marketing consultant.

Studying Your Competition

A consultant will study your competition for product offerings, service and convenience; as well as for sales volume and so on. They carry out this process by conducting the following:

Methods For Studying The Competition

1. *Visiting the business*
   (shopping the competition)
2. *Purchasing a product*
3. *Obtaining literature*
4. *Getting on their mailing list*
5. *Studying frequency of sales*
6. *Inquiring about pricing*
7. *Examining pricing structure*

Studying Clientele...

1. *Age*
2. *Sex*
3. *Ethnic background*
4. *Educational level*
5. *Marital and family status*
6. *Geographic location*
7. *Purchases: cash, credit, layaway*
8. *Frequency of purchases*

Studying Store Personnel

1. *Product knowledge*
2. *Willingness to service customers*
3. *General attitude concerning the business*
4. *Employees' interaction with one another*
5. *Grooming*

Store Image and Decor

1. *Are the internal and external images of the business consistent?*
2. *Does the decor coincide with the type of merchandise?*
3. *Is the lighting appropriate?*
4. *Does it arouse your interest?*
5. *Does it entice consumers to want to shop?*
6. *Can you clearly determine who they're trying to attract?*
7. *Is the store conveniently located?*
8. *How about business hours?*
9. *What services are offered...*
   A *Deferred payment plan*
   B. *Giveaways*
   C. *Coupons*
   D. *Discounts*
   E. *Free delivery*
   F. *Multiple purchase savings*
   G. *Gift wrapping*

The consultant would take initial steps to (1) Conduct a product and market analysis, (2) Review the needs of the potential customers, and (3) Select the attributes of the goods and services which fulfill the needs of the consumer.

Attracting Clients

Now that you have identified your market, studied your competition, and have a clear understanding of who your customer will be, you need to capture their attention. You must stimulate the desire of your prospective clients to conduct business with you. You must bring your goods and services to their attention.

Start with your immediate friends and family, business associates—anyone you can think of that would benefit from your services. Make a list of those individuals and send out announcements informing them of your new business venture. Don't hesitate to ask them for names of their friends and associates who might be interested in your services.

If you can, have a small grand opening for your business complete with samples of your work for review. It doesn't have to be elaborate, plan on some light refreshments. Enlist the services of your friends and family to model your garments. If you specialize in home decor, by all means have your home decorated in the best of your line. Take pictures of other projects that you have done in the past and have a small photo album available for show. How else can they think of employing your services, or recommend you to friends if they have no idea of what you can do?

If you specialize in children's clothing, contact child care centers and ask if you can leave your flyers and business cards. If you sew for special needs, contact those organizations that cater to those individuals.

If you specialize in costumes, contact your local high schools and colleges. Try and arrange an appointment to introduce your services to the head of the drama department.

If you enjoy home decor, contact realtors in your area and ask if they would be willing to refer clients to you; and offer to exchange leads. Better yet, contact the managers of local real estate offices and ask to give a brief presentation; leave flyers and business cards with each agent. It is not recommended that you contact new-home agents, as their companies generally have their own interior design centers. However, there is nothing stopping you from mailing flyers to new home buyers in the housing tract. If you feel exceptionally gregarious, you might canvass the area in person, introducing yourself and allowing them to preview your photo album of previous projects you have completed.

Alterations bring in a considerable income for those who enjoy this type of work. If this is your field of expertise, contact various cleaners and let them know that you specialize in alterations.

Another excellent way to attract clients is through beauty salons. They are a prime target for business. Most salons would be flattered to have a small fashion show. It is very elegant, and gives the salon a full-service appearance.

Consignment Agreement

While we are on the subject of beauty salons, ask the owner of a salon which you feel fits the image of your business if they would be interested in featuring your fashions, and offer them a small consignment fee for the use of their facility. Meet with the owner and work out the details. Make sure that you both understand your responsibilities as they relate to the garments and to the owner's salon.

Stipulate the beginning of the agreement, and how the agreement shall be terminated. Cover all concerns during your initial meeting prior to drafting the contract. Make it convenient for the owner of the salon; offer to draft the agreement. Draft a Consignment Agreement and have the owner sign followed by your signature; give the carbon copy to the owner. See the example on the following page.

Protect Yourself in a Consignment Agreement:

1. Have a signed contract
2. Use a control device - Inventory Sheet
3. Tag all garments
4. Get copies of all sales receipts
5. Collect all sales tax

CONSIGNMENT AGREEMENT

Per our conversation on_____,199_, I, your name_____
agree to place on consignment, articles of clothing & jewelry at
name of salon, located at address of salon, owned by owner of
salon.

I shall change the displays every two(2) weeks to maintain a
fresh appearance. I will not place holes or damage the walls of
the display area.

All articles of display such as hangers, visuals, etc, are the
sole property of your business name, and shall not be sold or
thrown away.

Each time articles are delivered to name of salon, I shall leave
an inventory sheet for control purposes only. All articles to be
sold will have inventory tags and shall be detached and given to
your name.

All proceeds from sales and sales tax, along with inventory tags,
inventory sheet, and a copy of sales receipt, shall be given to
your name.

A (15%) fifteen percent consignment fee shall be given to owners
name, owner and operator of name of salon. This fee is calculated
on gross sales minus sales tax. All sales tax shall be forwarded
to the State Board of Equalization by your name.

Any stolen, lost or damaged articles shall be the sole responsibility of_____.

Any changes, additions or amendments to this agreement shall be
submitted in writing and agreed upon by both parties, and shall
be added to the original agreement as Amendment A,B,C, etc.

date_____, is the date in which the first articles shall be
placed in name of salon, by your name__, and shall continue until
cancellation by either party.

____salon owner____   ____your signature____

date_____   date_____

A few points of major importance need to be discussed. First, the section in paragraph four of the Consignment Agreement regarding receipt of sales and taxes. You are responsible for reporting your taxes to the State Board; with this thought in mind, you must insure that you receive all funds generated from sales. Insist on getting a receipt of all sales. Tag all your clothing. You may make the tags or purchase them, either way will be effective. Each tag should have the following information: Code, Size, Price and Date Placed into inventory. See the bottom of the Pricing Sheet. The tag information will also appear on your Inventory Sheet. This sheet will be given to the salon owner. The Inventory Sheet is a control device and should not be overlooked. We shall review both the Inventory Sheet and the Pricing Sheet. First let's examine the Pricing Sheet.

Pricing Sheet

The Pricing Sheet is primarily used to help you establish a retail sales price for your items. However, it has many other uses. It insures that you do not overlook charging for materials and labor. It also helps to control fabric taken out of inventory for the production of garments, and further serves as a tracking device for all garments. For example, some sewing professionals make garments and put them on display in their studio. This is an excellent tool for repeat business. It gives clients ideas for future projects.

Notice that the "Status" line allows you to stipulate where the garment will be placed; either in a retail establishment or on display in your studio. The last section, "Tag Info" is where you

index the pertinent data that will go on the tag for
each garment. This applies to items placed into retail establishments. It also makes it easy to generate
an Inventory Sheet from the information in the "Tag
Info" section.

PRICING SHEET

ITEM_____

YARDS_____   PRICE PER YARD_____   TOTAL_____

FABRIC CODE_____   PATTERN #_____   PRICE_____

SIZE_____   LABOR HOURS_____

NOTIONS USED

THREAD_____   ELASTIC_____
INTERFACING_____   BUTTONS_____
CLOSURES_____   HEM TAPE
LINING_____   SHOULDER PADS_____
ZIPPER_____   BIAS TAPE_____
BONING_____   SLEEVE HEADS_____
PRESHRINKING_____   OTHER_____

TOTAL COST_____

MARKUP_____

RETAIL PRICE_____

COMPUTATION/NOTES

STATUS:_____RETAIL STORE____DISPLAY____

_____TAG INFO_____

CODE:

SIZE:

PRICE:

DATE:

Inventory Sheet

The Inventory Sheet can be made up from the tag information at the bottom of the Pricing Sheet. The Inventory Sheet informs the owner of the exact number of pieces you have placed into their establishment for sale. You might suggest to the salon owner that as the items are sold, it would be a good idea to highlight that particular line to reflect that the item is no longer included as part of the inventory count.

Making an Inventory Sheet is relatively easy. An example can be found on the next page. Start by establishing a coding system for each style. This will have been done on the Pricing Sheet. However, let's see how the coding process works.

If you will recall, in the chapter pertaining to financial planning, we discussed inventory methods utilized to keep track of fabric. This was accomplished by assigning codes to each fabric. Now you will see why this method is so beneficial. Look at lines eight and nine of the Inventory Sheet (Wearable Art Jkt/Top-Pant). You will notice that under "Style," there are a series of numbers and letters; the 80 & 81 and the 5F represent the code assigned to each fabric used to make this garment. The B3703/4481 stands for the patterns. The "B" is the code for the pattern used. The numbers indicate the actual number of each pattern.

The Inventory Sheet is helpful in many ways. For example, let's say you find that you receive a number of requests for a particular garment. You

can track the fabric and the patterns used by reviewing the inventory sheet. You may find that one
style or fabric sells extremely well; consequently,
this would be an indication that you should consider reproducing that particular garment.

INVENTORY SHEET

CUSTOM TAILORED CLOTHING

STYLE	DESCRIPTION	PCS	SIZE	PRICE
3CAPE91	GOLD/CAPE	1	ALL	69.00
577664V	BLACK DRESS	1	7	65.00
BUR3/91	WHITE DRESS	1	M	49.00
MAR/ART	FUS-JKT/WHT SATIN DRSE	2	7	150.00
80/82-V7941/2383	JKT/DRESS FUS/PUR.	2	M	89.00
52-V7635	DRESS/CAPE SHOULDER	1	S-M	85.00
80-81-5F-B3703/4481	WEARABLE ART JKT/TOP-PANT (FUS/PUR/GOLD)	3	S-M	118.00
24-3506B	DRESS,NUTMEG-BROWN	1	10	69.00
2FT6985B	TEDDY RED/WHT DOT	1	S	30.00
2FC6985B	CAMISOLE " "	2	M	40.00
2FR6985B	ROBE/SHORT " "	1	ALL	30.00
3F4905B	SUIT/RED	2	10	85.00
4F3506B	DRESS/WHITE/HEART BTNS	1	M	60.00

TOTAL PIECES (19)

NOTES:

Think of all the possible ways you can get your message to the consumer. We have discussed the more non-traditional methods of attracting clients and increasing business. You would be surprised at how effective non-traditional methods of marketing can be.

The more traditional methods would be to place your business cards into a card file at several local fabric stores, or call and make an appointment with the store manager. Be sure to take a sample of your work and ask for their support. I have enjoyed tremendous success through the support of *House of Fabrics*. They allowed flyers in clear lucite stands to be displayed near their cash registers. This is an excellent point-of-purchase display. A good number of individuals who shop fabric stores cannot sew, and are eager to find a good sewing professional. You would not believe the number of calls that were generated from this form of advertisement.

The fabric stores who were supportive to my business received flowers periodically during the year, and letters were sent to the managers thanking them for their support.

Clients who needed to purchase fabric and notions were referred to the fabric stores that supported my business. A business card was given to the client suggesting that they employ the assistance of the manager, and use my business card as a form of introduction. This demonstrates to the manager that you are supporting their store by referring your clients. Once you have established a good rapport, the sales staff and the manager are more inclined to refer clients to you.

It's not always easy to get stores to agree to this type of policy, as they are concerned with having to extend the same type of service to the many other sewing professionals, which could result in their counters looking very cluttered. However, you will never know unless you ask.

Another excellent way to attract clients is through networking with other sewing professionals. Engage in referring clients to your network associates whose needs do not match your field of specialty. Be sure to ask your fellow sewing professionals for referrals in return.

The above methods are cost effective, as they require little or no capital investment. Let's examine the more traditional methods of attracting clients through promotions and advertising.

Promotion and Advertising

Before spending a great deal of time and money on traditional advertisement and promotions, you must exhaust all non-traditional forms of marketing your business.

Placing advertisements into newspapers can be very expensive and can rob you of needed capital. You will have to measure the return on your investment prior to placing the advertisement.

Have the newspaper send you their media kit. A media kit will explain the type of clientele the paper targets, their readership, and many other pieces of valuable information you should know. Before investing precious capital into any ad campaign, make sure it is reaching your potential clientele. If it is not, you will be wasting good money on the wrong type of advertisement.

Before selecting any type of advertisement campaign, you need to determine the cost per thousand people your add will be exposed to. This is known as the *CPM*. Prior to placing any advertisement, be it newspaper, magazine, television, radio, or mailing out flyers through direct mail; calculate your CPM. How many clients would you need in order to recapture your advertising dollars is your major concern? If you can generate enough to cover the costs, you might consider placing the advertisement. Ask for any promotional or special discounts the company has to offer, and check to see if they offer any frequency discounts. Those are discounts available for placing a number of consecutive advertisements. Also, you can cut the cost of your advertising budget if you take advantage of co-op advertising with fellow sewing professionals.

Call the owners of sewing machine sales and service shops, since they generally have newsletters, sewing clubs, and mailing lists that you might be able to take advantage of. You will find advertising with them is far less expensive. This particular method works best if you are offering sewing lessons, or if you offer consultation to sewing professionals... it is an excellent way of getting your message across.

Check with the Chamber of Commerce or any community facility that places neighborhood advertisements, and ask about their requirements and rates.

If you plan to have giveaways for promotional consideration, be certain to analyze the cost-effectiveness first. How much of your profit margin will be affected by this type of promotional campaign? What will be the return on your investment?

Also, check the *Encyclopedia of Associations* to find organizations that would benefit from your services, and send letters to them asking if they have a mailing list that you could rent, or if they have a newsletter in which you might advertise.

For instance, if you are specializing in custom tailoring and you want to reach professional business women in your community, you could either rent the list for mass mailing purposes, or place a nice advertisement to attract their members. You also might offer to give a free fashion show. Some clubs are so prominent that they garner attention just by who they are. If you happen to be affiliated with this type of organization and are giving a fashion show, don't pass up the opportunity to get free publicity by sending a news release to your local newspaper. Editors are looking for good human interest stories to bring to their readers. Think like big businesses—promote, promote, promote!

The whole idea behind advertising and promotions is to gain the maximum from your efforts with the least amount of funds being taken away from your profits. Keep your mind open to new opportunities to attract clients and market your business.

If you have interesting advertisement and promotional methods you would like to share, please write the author at:

Barbara Wright Sykes
c/o Collins Publications
3233 Grand Avenue Suite N-294
Chino Hills, CA 91709

Custom
Tailoring

"Expanding Your Business"

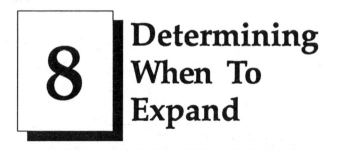

8 Determining When To Expand

Most entrepreneurs think of business expansion only in terms of moving to a new and larger location. Business expansion can take on many forms. You can expand your business by offering additional goods and services, or by hiring employees. Another possibility would be to subcontract out work, and the most common would be increasing size through a new or additional location. Let's take a look at each.

Goods and Services

You may be able to increase your clientele through additional product offerings. Let's say that you operate a bridal salon and you decide to add a tuxedo section. This would increase your business by making it a one-stop shopping center to the bridal party.

You might consider piggy-backing with other services related to your market. Negotiate a referral fee to generate additional revenue. You could start by having a photographer or limousine service display their brochures, and branch out from there. Draft a referral agreement and announce to the public that you now offer these new services.

There are a great number of ways to increase product and service offerings that will yield significant profits. Make sure that you keep all goods and services compatible with your business. You must consider your image, and who your customer is. Prior to instituting any new endeavor, you will have to study the market to insure there is a need. Be diligent and do your homework. Consider how much it will cost you and what will be the return on your investment.

Location

The only reason you might consider moving to another location for a home-based business would be if it was too much of an interruption on your family or, if your business increased to the point you outgrew your home and needed a larger, commercial-type setting.

A word of caution regarding commercial locations: It is not as simple as you might think. There are a number of legal ramifications involved. There are also costs associated with such an endeavor, such as percentage rents, maintenance, association fees, and so on.

Before going forward, you need to enlist the advice of your bookkeeper or accountant. The question of feasibility should be uppermost in your mind. You'll need to consider whether or not the location will be convenient for your present clientele. Will you need to hire employees? Your clientele must grow in order to cover the increased overhead associated with a retail location.

You will need answers to such questions as: Will the new location provide enough foot traffic to keep your business healthy? Are there individuals frequenting the existing establishments that could possibly be your future clients? Are the entrance and exit to the center convenient for clients? What about parking? Do they keep the facility clean? Spend some time observing the new site to make sure it is right for your business.

When considering a location, look for strong anchor tenants. An anchor tenant is one that is easily recognizable such as a Ralph's Grocery Store, or a May Company Department Store. They are businesses that most people have a need for. Large anchor tenants generally have substantial advertising campaigns and advertise on a regular basis. Neighboring businesses in the center will benefit from the increased foot traffic brought on as a result of advertising and promotions done by the anchor tenants.

Some leases require you to pay a percentage of your gross sales, and to belong to an association. You will need to have your attorney look them over, and in some cases, negotiate good terms for you. There is a lot of legal jargon that you may not be familiar with and your attorney will be able to decipher the contract for you.

If you decide to go this route, be sure to get an Exclusive. An Exclusive protects your business from competitors coming into your center. In other words, it protects you from a similar business moving in on your territory.

In summary, think of relocating your business as starting over—you will need to develop a new Business Plan. Refer to Chapter 4 and repeat your initial steps, thus insuring that you don't overlook anything.

Employees

Having employees can be quite complicated; there are many rules and regulations that must be followed, and you will have increased paper work keeping up with their time and performance.

You will need to determine if it will be advantageous for your business to expand by hiring employees. Look at the cost and compare it against the increased profit an employee will bring your business.

The federal government requires that you have an Employer Identification Number if you hire employees, or if the form of your business happens to be a partnership or corporation. Prior to hiring employees, you should contact the Internal Revenue Service for "Your Business Tax Kit." To obtain a free kit you may write to: **Internal Revenue Service, WADC, Rancho Cordova, CA 95743-0001**

To determine the prospective employee's qualifications, have them complete a thorough application. It would be a good idea to see their work also. This will give you an accurate picture of their skill level. You can purchase application forms from your local stationery store or make your own. The following is an example of a customized application.

EMPLOYMENT APPLICATION

NAME   DATE
ADDRESS
CITY   STATE   ZIP
PHONE   SOC. SEC#
PERSON TO CONTACT IN CASE OF EMERGENCY:

HIGH SCHOOL   COLLEGE   DEGREE
ON A SEPARATE SHEET OF PAPER ANSWER THE FOLLOWING QUESTIONS:

1. ARE YOU CURRENTLY EMPLOYED? WITH WHOM? INCLUDE ADDRESS AND TELEPHONE NUMBER. MAY WE CONTACT ALL OF YOUR EMPLOYERS?
2. LIST PAST 3 EMPLOYERS, POSITION HELD, DATES, SALARY, DESCRIBE RESPONSIBILITIES, REASON FOR LEAVING?
3. LIST COURSES TAKEN RELATED TO SEWING AND WHERE TAKEN.
4. WHAT DO YOU LIKE MOST ABOUT SEWING? WHAT DO YOU LIKE LEAST?
5. HOW DO YOU MAKE A LINING PATTERN FOR A BLAZER?
6. DO YOU KNOW THE PIVOT AND SLIDE METHOD OF ALTERING PATTERNS?
7. CAN YOU DRAFT A PATTERN?
8. WHAT TYPE OF SEWING MACHINES CAN YOU OPERATE? SERGERS?
9. HOW OFTEN SHOULD MACHINES BE CLEANED?
10. WHAT TYPE OF THREAD DO YOU USE?
11. LIST THREE ZIPPER APPLICATIONS.
12. DEFINE: TOPSTITCHING, UNDERSTITCHING, STAYSTITCHING
13. WHAT IS PRE-SHRINKING?
14. HOW WOULD YOU PRE-SHIRINK THE FOLLOWING:
    1)WOOL   2)SILK   3)COTTON   4)LINEN
15. WHAT IS THE DIFFERENCE BETWEEN WOVEN AND KNIT FABRICS?
17. CAN YOU MATCH PLAIDS AND STRIPES?
18. DO YOU KNOW THE METRIC SYSTEM? ARE YOU GOOD WITH FRACTIONS?
19. HOW LONG DOES IT TAKE YOU TO COMPLETE THE FOLLOWING:
    1)SKIRT   2)BLOUSE   3)JACKET/BLAZER   4)DRESS
20. DO YOU PRESS AS YOU CONSTRUCT THE GARMENT?
21. WHEN DO YOU USE UNDERLINING?
22. LIST THE DIFFERENT TYPES OF SEAM FINISHES.
23. ARE YOU FAMILIAR WITH: 1) FRONT FLY ZIPPERS
    2)COVERED BUTTONS   3)BOUND BUTTON HOLES   4)WELT POCKETS
24. CAN YOU MAKE SHOULDER PADS?
25. HOW DO YOU APPLY FUSIBLE INTERFACING TO FABRIC?
26. BRIEFLY DESCRIBE YOUR FITTING TECHNIQUES?
27. BRIEFLY DESCRIBE YOUR DESIGN SKILLS?
28. WHAT ARE YOUR STRONG POINTS RELATED TO THIS POSITION?
29. WHAT ARE YOUR AVAILABLE HOURS? DAYS?
30. WHAT HOURLY RATE DO YOU DESIRE?
31. DO YOU PREFER WORKING IN YOUR HOME?
32. WILL YOU NEED ANY SPECIAL TIME OFF DURING THE YEAR?
33. WHEN CAN YOU START?

SIGNATURE_____

Subcontracting

One of the best ways to expand your business without incurring expenses is to hire subcontractors. This will allow you to maintain your home-based business—and your privacy. The subcontractors will perform the work in their home or place of business.

Just as you would an employee, you need to discover the skill level of the subcontractor. Have them bring samples of their work, and a listing of clients they have worked for. Be sure to follow through and check their references. You need insurance that this person can meet deadlines and will be committed to their work.

Make a list of questions you wish to cover prior to the face-to-face interview. You should conduct the interview somewhat the same way you would for hiring an employee. Make sure you have gotten satisfactory answers to all of your questions prior to discussing the contract.

One pertinent question that always reveals a great deal about the applicant is "What are your expectations of this job?"

You want to know why they desire to work for you. When you feel reasonably sure the applicant is someone who meets your standards, introduce the subject of the contract. A sample contract is given in the following example:

INDEPENDENT CONTRACTORS AGREEMENT

THE FOLLOWING IS A CONTRACT FOR SEWING SERVICES BETWEEN
_____AND_____ .
EFFECTIVE _____, 199__.

SERVICES TO BE PROVIDED ARE THOSE NEEDED TO CUT, SEW, CONSTRUCT,
PRESS, AND ALTER VARIOUS GARMENTS.

GARMENTS WILL BE PICKED UP AND DELIVERED AT _____,
LOCATED AT:_____

ALL GARMENTS WILL HAVE WORK ORDERS ATTACHED STIPULATING CLIENT,
WORK TO BE COMPLETED, FABRIC/NOTIONS INCLUDED, AND DATE DUE.

GARMENTS ARE TO BE RETURNED WITH ALL NOTIONS, THREADS, PATTERNS,
FABRIC, INTERFACING, (INCLUDING SCRAPS), ON DUE DATE.

WORK ORDERS ARE TO BE RETURNED WITH ALL GARMENTS INDICATING WORK
COMPLETED AND NOTED ON THE PATTERN ADJUSTMENT CHECK LIST.

INDEPENDENT SEAMSTRESS _____, IS
RESPONSIBLE FOR ALL DAMAGED, LOST, OR STOLEN MERCHANDISE.

PAY SCHEDULES WILL BE _____,
AND WILL COVER ALL WORK COMPLETED TO DATE.

STANDARDS OF QUALITY REGARDING PRODUCTION, SEWING, CUTTING,
PRESSING, CONSTRUCTION AND ALTERATIONS WILL BE MAINTAINED,
REVIEWED AND DISCUSSED DURING THE LIFE OF THIS CONTRACT.

FEES FOR SERVICES RENDERED ARE AS FOLLOWS:

SEE ATTACHED FEE SCHEDULE

TERMINATION OF THIS AGREEMENT MUST OCCUR TWO WEEKS PRIOR TO THE
DATE OF ACTUAL TERMINATION AND MUST BE SUBMITTED IN WRITING BY
EITHER PARTIES.

PRIOR TO TERMINATION ALL FEES OWED TO_____
_____ MUST BE PAID IN
FULL; LIKEWISE ALL NOTIONS, PATTERNS, FABRICS, THREAD, GARMENTS
AND/OR PROPERTY, SHALL BE RETURNED TO:

_____

SIGNATURE_____DATE_____

SIGNATURE_____DATE_____

"Expanding Your Professional Talents"

9 | Expanding Your Professional Talents

Teaching

Many successful entrepreneurs engage in other sources of revenue-producing ventures; generally, they relate to one another. For instance, a chef at a restaurant might engage in teaching culinary arts at a trade college.

Conversely, a sewing professional would engage in teaching sewing either privately or by group, or both. The field chosen should be directly related to sewing itself. More often than not, you will be qualified to utilize your talents in other income-producing endeavors.

Fees

When establishing fees, you must first consider whether you will be teaching private lessons or group. If you are going to teach group lessons, you could pass on a discount for specific numbers enrolled.

In computing your fees, you must keep in mind

what your goal is for earning a monthly salary. The fees you charge must coincide with your goal. For example, if you need to earn one hundred dollars a day to reach your goal, you must charge fees for your time that will yield those results.

Other fees or expenses must be factored in or charged directly to the student. If you teach in your studio, you must allow for upkeep and maintenance of your machines. A machine usage fee is ideal to cover these costs, and the cost of needles and other necessities. If you provide handouts, figure the cost into your price, or charge the fee directly to the student for supplies.

Mileage is an overlooked expense by a number of professionals. It shouldn't be, if a student wishes to have private lessons in their home. It will cost you money for gas in order to accommodate their wishes. You must calculate what the cost per mile would be and make a mileage chart. Refer to the mileage fees on the Sample Price List in Chapter 5.

Forms

For your teaching business, you will need to develop two basic business forms: (1) the Sewing Lessons Contract, and (2) the Rules and Regulations by which you will govern your classes. All other forms will be generic to the subject matter being taught. Following are examples of the two basic forms:

SEWING LESSONS CONTRACT

SECTION I

STUDENT NAME_____DATE_____
BIRTHDAY_____REFERRED BY_____
ADDRESS_____
CITY_____ZIP_____
HOME PHONE_____WORK_____

PERSON TO CONTACT IN CASE OF AN EMERGENCY
NAME_____RELATIONSHIP_____
ADDRESS_____PHONE_____

RULES AND REGULATIONS RECEIVED/ACKNOWLEDGED_____
STUDENT SIGNATURE_____

STUDENTS UNDER AGE 18 NEED PARENT/GUARDIANS CONSENT
PERMISSION GRANTED BY_____
                     (PARENT/GUARDIAN)

OFFICE USE

PRIVATE____GROUP____PLACE_____

NUMBER OF LESSONS_____   FEE_____
MACHINE FEE_____   MILEAGE_____
SUPPLIES_____   TOTAL FEES_____
PAID_____   START DATE_____

DATES_____TIME_____
       _____   _____
       _____   _____
       _____

SECTION II

ADDITIONAL LESSONS

PERMISSION GRANTED BY_____
DATE_____   (PARENT/GUARDIAN)

NUMBER OF LESSONS_____   FEE_____
TOTAL_____PAID_____   START DATE_____
DATES   TIME
       _____   _____
       _____   _____

I ACCEPT FULL FINANCIAL RESPONSIBILITY FOR ALL LESSONS
AGREED UPON IN THIS CONTRACT.

SIGN_____DATE_____

SEWING CLASS RULES/REGULATIONS

1. STUDENTS ARE TO BE PRESENT AND ON TIME TO ALL CLASSES SCHEDULED.

2. IF A CLASS IS MISSED WITHOUT CALLING AHEAD A $10.00 MISSED FEE SHALL BE CHARGED FOR EACH OCCURRENCE.

3. ALL OUTSIDE ASSIGNMENTS ARE TO BE COMPLETED ON TIME, AND READY FOR REVIEW AT THE BEGINNING OF CLASS.

4. THERE IS A $10.00 SEWING MACHINE USAGE FEE FOR THOSE STUDENTS ELECTING TO USE STUDIO SEWING MACHINES.

5. WE ACCEPT NO LIABILITY FOR MACHINES, MATERIALS OR OTHER EQUIPMENT BROUGHT TO THE STUDIO FOR USE BY THE STUDENT DURING SCHEDULED LESSONS.

6. LESSONS ARE TO BE PAID FOR IN ADVANCE.

7. MILEAGE FEES ARE TO BE PAID FOR IN ADVANCE.

8. STUDENTS ARE RESPONSIBLE FOR CLEANING HIS/HER OWN WORK AREA BEFORE LEAVING CLASS.

9. ALL SEWING NOTIONS, MATERIALS AND EQUIPMENT SHALL BE LABELED BY STUDENT TO AVOID CONFUSION.

PINS	PIN CUSHION
TAPE MEASURE-60 INCHES	SHEARS (SCISSORS)
MARKING PENCIL	SEAM RIPPER
HAND SEWING NEEDLES	6 INCH GAUGE
BOX/BASKET FOR NOTIONS	TRACING PAPER
TRACING WHEEL (SMOOTH)	PENCIL/PAPER

IN ADDITION TO THE ABOVE ITEMS A SUITABLE PATTERN, FABRIC, AND NOTIONS WILL BE DISCUSSED AND APPROVED PRIOR TO THE FIRST LESSON.

I_____, HAVE READ AND UNDERSTAND THE ABOVE RULES/REGULATIONS, AND AGREE TO THE TERMS AND CONDITIONS SET FORTH.

Teaching Materials

The major pattern companies are advocates of continuing education. Many of them have full-time education departments specifically designed to promote continuing education in the field of sewing.

They produce wonderful teaching aids that cost very little. In some cases they even provide certain literature free to schools and teachers. As an instructor, I have relied upon the many helpful educational materials available from the leading pattern companies. The students find them extremely helpful, and for teachers, they are excellent tools to add spice to a lesson plan. Listed below are the addresses of the leading pattern companies. Write to them and request information on materials available for teachers.

Mc Call's Pattern Co.
1110 Penn Plaza
New York, NY 10001

Simplicity Pattern Co.
200 Madison Ave., 5th Floor
New York, NY 10016

NOTE: Simplicity also carries
New Look and Style patterns

Butterick/Vogue
161 Avenue of the Americas
New York, NY 10013

Burda Patterns
P.O. Box 670628
Marietta, GA 30066

Seminars

Seminars are a wonderful way to earn extra income. Get acquainted with different clubs such as the Bernina Club. Contact different sewing machine sales and service centers, and introduce yourself. Explain your qualifications, discuss the possibility of your conducting a seminar. Contact fabric stores, trade associations, sewing guilds, and network organizations. These groups enjoy seminars on timely topics related to sewing. Explore all possibilities and follow through.

Writing Articles

If you are good at teaching, conducting seminars, or you are extremely knowledgeable in your craft, chances are you would be very good at writing articles for trade publications. It is a rewarding experience to have your first "by line" and to see your name in print, in addition to sharing your knowledge with others.

Practice writing a few articles and have them reviewed by a professional for content and style as well as for grammar and punctuation. To gain experience and confidence, you might try writing for a sewing club as a volunteer for a short time. Once you feel secure, submit your work to editors of leading sewing publications.

Books/Videos

Two excellent learning tools that are utilized by schools as well as consumers are books and video tapes. What better way to learn than through the written word and visual communication? Just as with writing articles, there are a number of individuals who could benefit from your knowledge.

If you want to star in your own video, you should write an outline of the subject matter you wish to convey. If you can't think of material, follow the suggestions in the following paragraph.

For a video, you will need to write a script, so why not spend the time writing a book as a companion piece to the video, which can be translated into a script? You will be doing extensive writing anyway, this way it will bring double benefits.

Most videos originate from books and are transformed into the script. You will need to hire a professional script writer. Writing a script is completely different from a book. Don't risk the quality of the video by not hiring a professional.

List your skills and areas of expertise. Ask someone in your profession what they would like to know more about. If you belong to a network group or professional organization, conduct a survey through the uses of a questionnaire. Once it is completed, compile the data for review. If you discover a void that needs to be filled, start your research so that *you* can be the one to fill it!

As you have discovered, there are a number of avenues available for you to expand your professional talents.

If writing articles and books or starring in your very own video appeals to you; for further information send a legal size, self-addressed stamped envelope to:

Collins Publications
Media Information
3233 Grand Avenue Suite N-294
Chino Hills, CA 91709

10 Determination Equals Success!

You Are A Winner

There is a winner in everyone. All you have to do is unleash the powers that be. You have been gifted with sewing talents, and now you must put them to work for you.

Many successful individuals have started from square one. Use the principles set forth in each chapter of this text as a guide, and above all—remember to believe in yourself and your ability to succeed. Be determined. I live by the motto "Determination Equals Success!"

I welcome your letters and comments. If you wish to consult with me, please send a legal self-addressed stamped envelope to:

BARBARA WRIGHT AND ASSOCIATES
c/o COLLINS PUBLICATIONS
ATTN: BARBARA WRIGHT SYKES
3233 GRAND AVENUE, SUITE N-294
CHINO HILLS, CA 91709

Author's Profile

Barbara Wright Sykes maintains a successful custom tailoring business which affords her the luxury to utilize her creative talents regularly. Her fashions have been featured in major retail establishments.

She teaches sewing to a vast array of skill levels, from the beginner to the more advanced. She is a frequent guest speaker at sewing clubs and organizations. She has also appeared on cable television and local radio shows, and has several articles written about her. In addition, she has just completed the cover layout for a national education and employment magazine.

For a number of years, she consulted with a variety of businesses under her firm's name, Barbara Wright and Associates. At present, she consults exclusively with sewing enthusiasts and professionals who either want to go into business, or those who are in business and are experiencing difficulty.

Her previous experience includes being the owner of her own clothing store, "Elegance In Vogue," and teaching business and career development at a local business college, for which she received an Outstanding Teachers Award. She has two degrees, one in accounting and a second in business education with an emphasis in marketing.

She has been sewing for approximately thirty-five years and has taken numerous sewing and tailoring classes and studied commercial techniques under one of the industries' leaders. In essence, she has combined her two loves into one, her love of business and her love of sewing; to make her dream come true...and she continues to live by her belief that "Determination Equals Success!"

Appendix

BOOKS/BIBLIOGRAPHY

BUSINESS

ENTREPRENEURIAL MOTHERS, Phyllis Gillis, *Rawson Associates*, 1984

LEVERAGED FINANCE: HOW TO RAISE AND INVEST CASH, Mark Stevens, Prentice-Hall, Inc., 1981

PAST DUE: HOW TO COLLECT MONEY, Norman King, Facts On File, 1983

PRICE IT RIGHT, Claire Shaeffer, Box 157, Palm Springs, CA 92663; 1984

SEW TO SUCCESS, Kathleen Spike, Palmer/Pletcsh, 1990

SEWING AS A BUSINESS, Beth Duncan, Publicaton No. 1667, Mississippi Cooperative Service, PO Box 5446, Mississippi State, MS 39762

SEWING AS A HOME BUSINESS, Mary Roehr, 3597 Vicksburg Ct., Tallahasee, FL 32308; 1983

START-UP MONEY, Mike P. McKeever, Nolo Press, 1986

WORKING FOR YOURSELF, Phillip Namanworth and Gene Busnar, McGraw-Hill, 1985

MOTIVATIONAL AUDIO TAPES

HOW TO BE A WINNER, Zig Ziglar, Nightingale-Conant Corp.

IT'S TIME FOR YOU, Rita Davenport, P.O. Box 11932, Phoenix, Arizona 85061

THE POWER OF POSITIVE THINKING, Dr. Norman Vincent Peale, Simon & Schuster

SEWING

DRESSMAKING WITH SPECIAL FABRICS, Rosalie Giles, Bell & Hyman, 1982

FABRIC SEWING GUIDE, Claire Shaeffer, Chilton, 1989

NEEDLE KNOWS ABOUT ULTRASUEDE, Joan Kunze, Phillips, and Jean Kunze Sullivan, Needle Knows, 1982

POWER SEWING, Sandra Betzina, 95 Fifth Ave., San Francisco, CA 94118, 1985

SENSATIONAL SILK, Gail Brown, Palmer/Pletsch, 1982

SEW A BEAUTIFUL WEDDING, Gail Brown, Palmer/Pletsch, 1980

SILKS'N SATINS, Hazel Boyd, Tex-Mar Seminars and Publications, 1986

THE BUSY WOMAN'S SEWING BOOK, Robbie Fanning and Nancy Zieman, Open Chain Publishing, 1988

THE DRESSMAKER'S DICTIONARY, Ann Ladbury, Arco Publishing, Inc., 1982

FAIRCHILD BOOKS, Phone (800) 247-6622
- *The Art of Fashion Draping*
- *Basic Pattern Skills for Fashion Design*
- *Childrenswear Design*
- *Classic Tailoring Techniques/Men's*
- *Classic Tailoring Techniques/Women's*
- *Fabulous Fit*
- *Fashion Design for the Plus Size*
- *Fitting and Pattern Alteration*

SEWING ROOM DESIGN AND LAYOUT

Organize Your Sewing Area, Nancy's Notions, 800-833-0690 (Ask for the video and transcript)

Trends In Sewing Room Design, Palmer/Pletsch, 503-274-0687 (Ask for Bulletin No.1)

FIGURE ANALYSIS AND STYLE (Videos)

BODY SHAPES AND SILHOUETTES, Burda Patterns, (See Resource Guide)

FITTING FOR STYLE, Nancy Zieman, Nancy's Notions, (See Resource Guide)

FLATTER YOUR FIGURE, Jan Larkey, Has a companion Book. Both may be ordered through Nancy's Notions. (See Resource Guide)

MISCELLANEOUS

DESIGN WITHOUT LIMITS: DESIGNING AND SEWING FOR SPECIAL NEEDS, Simplicity Pattern Co., (See Resource Guide)

RESOURCE GUIDE

REFERENCE BOOKS

Books In Print, Lists all current books by suject, title and author.
Directories in Print, Lists specialized directories.
Encyclopedia of Associations, List names of professional organizations.
Forthcoming Books, Future books scheduled to appear in Books In Print.
Newsletters in Print, List published newsletters
Paperback Books in Print, List paperback books by subject, title and author.

MAGAZINES/NEWSLETTERS

Butterick, PO Box 569, Altoona, PA 16603-9974
McCalls Patterns, PO Box 3325, Manhattan, KS 66502-9917
Serger Update, Update Newsletters, PO Box 5029, Harlan, IA 51593
Sew News, PJS Publications, Inc., PO Box 1790, Peoria, IL 61656
Sewing Update, Update Newsletters, PO Box 5029, Harlan, IA 51593
The Creative Machine, Open Chain Publishing Co., PO Box 2634-NL, Menlo Park, CA 94026 (Newsletter)
Threads, The Taunton Press, PO Box 5506, Newton, CT 06470-9976
Vogue Patterns, PO Box 751, Altoona, PA 16003

SEWING ORGANIZATIONS

American Sewing Guild, PO Box 50976, Indianapolis, Indiana 46250-5976
Professional Association Of Custom Clothiers, (PACC), 1375 Broadway, 4th Floor, New York, NY 10018
SewCiety, E. Ann Riegel, c/o Baby Lock U.S.A., P.O. Box 730, Fenton, MO 63026-0730

NOTIONS, BOOKS, AND TAPES

Clotilde Inc., 1909 S.W. First Ave., Fort Lauderale, FL 33315, Phone 305-761-8655

Collins Publications, 3233 Grand Ave., Suite N-294, Chino Hills, CA 91709

Fairchild Books, Marketing Dept., 7 West 34th St., New York, NY 10001, Phone 800-247-6622

Fit For You, 781 Golden Prados Drive, Diamond Bar, CA 91765

Nancy's Notions, 333 Beichl Ave., PO Box 683, Beaver Dam, WI 53916-0683, Phone 800-833-0690

The Sewing Connection, 922 Chiltenham Way, Plainfield, IN 46168

PATTERN COMPANIES

Mc Call's Pattern Co.
1110 Penn Plaza
New York, NY 10001

Simplicity Pattern Co.
200 Madison Ave., 5th Floor
New York, NY 10016
NOTE: Simplicity also carries
New Look and **Style** patterns

Butterick/Vogue
161 Avenue of the Americas
New York, NY 10013

Burda Patterns
P.O. Box 670628
Marietta, GA 30066

SOFTWARE & TUTORIALS

LearnKey, 93 S. Mountain Way Dr., Box F, Orem, UT 84058 Phone 800-937-3279 (Tutorial)

Livingsoft, Inc., 524 West Dolphen St., Ridgecrest, CA 93555 Phone 800-626-1262 (Pattern Making Software)

WHOLESALE DISTRIBUTORS

Lions Notions Inc.
1260 North Lakeview Ave.
Anaheim, CA 92807
Phone 800-222-0288
or 714-693-0560

Tacony Corporation
1760 Gilsinn Lane
Fenton, MO 63026
Fax 314-349-2333
Phone 800-482-2669

MISCELLANEOUS

Copyright Office
Library of Congress
Washington, D.C. 20559

Patent & Trademark Office
U.S. Dept. of Commerce
Washington, D.C. 20231

Small Business Administration (SBA)
SBA Answer Desk in Washington, D.C, Call 800-368-5855

Ask about the following:

1) Score Counselors
3) SBA Publications

2) Pre-Business Workshops
4) Other services available

Internal Revenue Service
WADC
Rancho Cordova, CA 95743-0001
Ask for "Your Business Tax Kit"

INDEX

Also From Collins Publications

Overcoming Doubt, Fear And Procrastination, by Barbara Wright Sykes. There are three common enemies that will rob you of achieving your success: Doubt, Fear and Procrastination. By following Barbara Wright Sykes' five-step approach, you will conquer the demons that have kept you from having the happy, prosperous life you deserve! Barbara takes you into the lives of successful people, as they share with you the real glue that held them together as they triumphed over doubt, fear and procrastination. This book can change your life and will assist you in reaching your goals and living up to your full potential, for a little of your time and only $24.95!

Overcoming Doubt, Fear And Procrastination Workbook, by Barbara Wright Sykes. Put everything you learn from the book into practice by implementing the techniques in the workbook. A magnificent way to put a prevent doubt, fear and procrastination. There is no stopping you now! And for the small price of only $9.95!

Secrets Of Personal Marketing Power: *Strategies for Achieving Greater Personal & Business Success,* by Don L. Price. This book will increase your knowledge, sharpen your skills in personal marketing, and focus your energies toward greater success! You will discover the effective principles and secret weapons of personal marketing power, plus, how to find and master your center of power! The cost of this dynamic key to success is only $19.95!

VIDEO AND CD-ROM TRAINING
Learn Computer Software & The Internet The Easy Way

➤ Word ➤ Excel ➤ PowerPoint Wordperfect ➤ WordPro ➤ MS Office
➤ Access ➤ Corel Draw ➤ Lotus Suite ➤ Windows NT Certification
➤ Doing Business On The Internet ➤ Internet Basics ➤ Windows ➤
➤ Novel Netware ➤ and many more call for free brochure!!
1-800-795-8999

To purchase the above books, please use the order form provided in this book, or call
1-800-795-8999. Please refer to the order form for shipping and handling costs.
Ask about our gift certificates! Prices are subject to change without notice.

Do You Sew For Profit?

Here is everything you need to achieve and maintain success!

The "Business" of Sewing Book is a comprehensive and informative guide or textbook. It offers a detailed analysis of pricing, business plans, financial planning, how to attract clients, sewing studio layout and design and more, all for only $14.95!

The "Business" of Sewing Audio Album consists of three cassettes: 1. *The "Business" of Sewing* features Barbara Wright Sykes live in one of her many sold-out seminar presentations, where she shares secrets to success as a sewing professional making $800 to $1,000 a day! 2. *Taking the Fear Out of Pricing*: No more under-charging. Discover how to get paid what you are worth through an in-depth study of pricing for profit. 3. *Marketing Your Sewing Business* explores successful marketing techniques to attract clients. Learn how to market your sewing talents and earn money as you sleep! This attractive and valuable audio album is only $45.00. **Individually, each cassette costs $16.95**.

Complete Set of Forms: 23 business forms, including price sheets, measurement charts, and more. You'll have all you will need to start, maintain and achieve success for only $30.00. Or, buy the same forms available as *Forms on Disk*, compatible with any program able to read WordPerfect files for just $35.99.

Dream Sewing Spaces, by Lynette Ranney Black. Make your dream sewing space a reality! In *Dream Sewing Spaces*, color photos of a wide variety of sewing spaces provide inspiration. Create your own sewing studio out of a wall in a hallway, a corner of your bedroom a niche in the kitchen, space in the attic, or a commercial location! This innovative book is a must for only $19.95!

Price It Right, by Claire Shaeffer. Setting a price for your time is never easy, it is especially difficult for sewing entrepreneurs. *Price It Right* is based on a collection of price lists that utilize an add-on unit system which reflects the time required, as well as the difficulty of each procedure. It begins with a base amount to which supplementary values are added for more complex garments, difficult fabrics, and extra services. It can be used for complete garment construction as well as alterations. Since this add-on unit system is not a dollar amount, it can be used by a dressmaker in rural America as well as Big City, USA, to establish prices today, tomorrow, or in the year 2,000. You can order it for only $10.00!

Sew To Success, by Kathleen Spike. Kathleen shares her knowledge and expertise on how to achieve success in a home-based sewing business. Included are sample forms, pricing methods, and much more, for only $10.95

The above may be purchased from the order form in this book, or you may call toll free **1-800-795-8999**. *Please refer to the order form for shipping and handling fees. Ask about our gift certificates! Prices subject to change without notice.*

COLLINS PUBLICATIONS Order Form   ☐SHIP ☐Regular ☐Airmail

TITLE	PRICE	QTY.	TOTAL	S
Book: *Overcoming Doubt, Fear & Procrastination*	$24.95			
Workbook: *Overcoming Doubt, Fear & Procrastination*	$10.00			
Book: *Secrets of Personal Marketing Power*	$19.95			
Book: *The "Business" of Sewing*	$14.95			
Audio Tape 1. The *"Business"* of Sewing	$16.95			
Audio Tape 2. *Taking The Fear Out Of Pricing*	$16.95			
Audio Tape 3. *Marketing Your Sewing Business*	$16.95			
The *"Business"* of Sewing Audio Album (3 cassettes: 1. The *"Business"* of Sewing; 2. Taking the Fear Out of Pricing; 3. Marketing Your Sewing Business)	$45.00			
Complete Set of Forms (The *"Business" of Sewing*)	$30.00			
Forms on Computer Disk (The *"Business"* of Sewing)	$35.99			
Demo Disk: Dress Shop 2.0	$5.00			
Book: *Sew to Success*	$10.95			
Book: *Price It Right*	$10.00			
Book: *Dream Sewing Spaces*	$19.95			
Back Issues of *The "Business" of Sewing* Newsletter. Specify issue desired when ordering ($2.00 per issue or all 7 for $12.00) off ea.) ☐Summer '93 ☐Fall '93 ☐Spring/Summer '94 ☐Fall '94 ☐Winter '94 ☐Fall '95 ☐Winter '95				
Mail order to: Collins Publications, 3233 Grand Ave., Suite N-294M, Chino Hills, CA 91709-1489	Subtotal			
Use state tax applicable	Tax			
US Shipping: Up to $25.....$4.75 $101 to $150........$10.70 $26 to $50..........................$6.70 $150 plus.............$12.70 $51 to $100......................$8.70 Add $2 Canada, $5 International	Shipping & Handling			
Regular shipping takes 3-5 weeks; Airmail takes 3-5 days	Add $1.95 Airmail			
Credit Card Orders 800-795-8999 FAX Orders 909-393-6217 Customer Service 909-606-1009	$1 Credit Card Processing Fee			
Prices Subject To Change Without Notice	TOTAL US FUNDS ONLY			

Date_____ Name_____

Home Phone_____ Work Phone_____

Address_____ City_____

State_____ Zip_____ ☐ Check #_____

☐Money Order   ☐Visa   ☐MasterCard   ☐American Express   ☐Cash $_____

Credit Card #_____ Exp. Date_____

Name on Card_____ Signature_____

Authorization_____ Reference_____

Special Offer

*Any back issue of The "Business" of Sewing Newsletter
for only $2.00 or all seven for only $12.00*

Winter 1995: Breaking The Rules With "Quik" Sewing Skills ▪ Tailoring With Mary Ellen Flurry Jacket Fitting Adjustments ▪ Computer News ▪ Little Tips For Big Projects ▪ Book Reviews New Money For Female Entrepreneur'S ▪ Fashion Forecast ▪ Sew Perfect ▪ Price It Right

Fall 1995: Niche Your Sewing Business: Sew For Children ▪ So, You Want To Teach Children To Sew ▪ Workroom Design: Space Solutions For Sewing Workrooms ▪ Make It Your Own Kids Are My Clients-And The Rewards Are Unlimited ▪ How To Preshirink Interfacing

Winter 1994: Dream Window Collections ▪ The Sewing Connection ▪ Bridal Forum ▪ Book Reviews ▪ Creative Keepsakes ▪ Bedroom Decorating-Create The Designer Look Here Comes The Bride ▪ Business And Tax Tips ▪ Christmas Decoration ▪ Business Weapons

Spring/Summer 1994: Sewing Offers Multifaceted Career ▪ Sewing Machines For The Nineties What Are The Elements Of A Good Contract ▪ Promotional Garments ▪ Barbara Wright Sykes Kathleen Spike Sews To Success ▪ The Couturiers Touch ▪ Combining Fashions & Graphics

Fall 1994: Studio Expansion Manageable And Rewarding ▪ Japanese Culture Influences Entrepreneur To Start Business ▪ Buttons From Earrings ▪ The Art Of African Fashions ▪ Mens Tailoring - From Livingroom To Showroom ▪ Personal Computers- The Rule Rather Than The Exception

Fall 1993: Japanese Tailoring ▪ Industrial Tips For Sewing Pros ▪ Turn Soda Bottles Into Fabric ▪ Pant Drafting ▪ Where Are All The Fabric Stores ▪ Featuring Nancy Zieman ▪ Know Your Legal Liability ▪ Portrait Of A Sewing Professional ▪ Computer Pattern Drafting ▪ Margaret Islander

Summer 1993: Power Sewing With Sandra Betzina ▪ Sewing Entrepreneur Finds Market Niche ▪ Tools For Business Start-Up And Recordkeeping ▪ Hiring Employees Or Independent Contractors ▪ Sales Tax Made Easier ▪ The Birth Of Dress Shop Software: Featuring Annette Schofield

---

Coming soon the Video, Audio and CD-ROM of...

Overcoming Doubt, Fear and Procrastination

call 1-800-795-8999